The Lessons of Tragedy

The Lessons of Tragedy

Statecraft and World Order

HAL BRANDS AND CHARLES EDEL

Yale UNIVERSITY PRESS

New Haven and London

Published with assistance from the income of the Frederick John
Kingsbury Memorial Fund.

Published with assistance from the foundation established in
memory of Philip Hamilton McMillan of the Class of 1894, Yale
College.

Yale University Press books may be purchased in quantity for
educational, business, or promotional use. For information, please
e-mail sales.press@yale.edu (U.S. office) or sales@yaleup.co.uk
(U.K. office).

Set in Minion type by IDS Infotech, Ltd.
Printed in the United States of America.

Library of Congress Control Number: 2018950176
ISBN 978-0-300-23824-2 (hardcover : alk. paper)

A catalogue record for this book is available from the British
Library.

This paper meets the requirements of ANSI/NISO Z39.48-1992
(Permanence of Paper).

10 9 8 7 6 5 4 3 2

For Henry and Annabelle and Caleb and Henry

Contents

Acknowledgments   ix

INTRODUCTION.   1

ONE. The Virtues of Tragedy   7

TWO. Tragedy as the Norm   22

THREE. Tragedy as Inspiration   41

FOUR. The Great Escape   64

FIVE. The Contemporary Amnesia   90

SIX. The Darkening Horizon   117

SEVEN. Rediscovering Tragedy   145

Notes   167
Index   193

Acknowledgments

This is a short book, but we have accumulated a long list of debts. For lending their time, expertise, and support, we would like to thank Ross Babbage, Jim Baker, Frances Brown, Eliot Cohen, Eric Crahan, Ron Daniels, Charlie Davis, Peter Dutton, Liz Economy, Eric Edelman, Jeffrey Engel, David Epstein, Andrew Erickson, Peter Feaver, John Lewis Gaddis, Patrick Gaughen, Frank Gavin, Simon Goldfine, Gorana Grgic, Toby Harshaw, Charlie Hill, Will Inboden, Simon Jackman, Colin Jackson, Donald Kagan, Colin Kahl, Paul Kennedy, Michael Kimmage, Thomas LeBien, Tom Mahnken, John Maurer, Andrew May, Walter Russell Mead, David Milne, Siddharth Mohandas, Jared Mondscheir, Michael Morgan, Vali Nasr, Aaron Nygunes, Aaron O'Connell, Michael O'Hara, Nikhil Patel, Mira Rapp-Hooper, Ely Ratner, Kori Schake, Drew Sheldrick, James Simpson, Jim Steinberg, Jeremi Suri, Adam Swaim, Julia Sweig, James Wilson, and Toshi Yoshihara. Whether they know it or not, this book was much enriched by their advice and support.

Having attended graduate school together, we were also lucky to end up working in government at the same time. Our experience there informed this book; we would like to thank the Council on Foreign Relations for making those experiences possible. We would also like to thank our institutional homes—the Johns Hopkins School of Advanced International Studies and the Center for Strategic and Budgetary Assessments for Hal, the U.S. Studies Centre at the University of Sydney for Charlie—for providing intellectually stimulating environments. Hal would particularly like to thank Pablo Scuticchio, Emily Hardman, and Brogan Ingstad for their assistance in researching the book.

At Yale University Press, Jaya Aninda Chatterjee was a pleasure to work with, and Dan Heaton and Joyce Ippolito helped steer the book through the production process. Our agent, Rafe Sagalyn, provided much helpful advice and assistance. We would also like to thank the anonymous reviewer who provided many thoughtful and encouraging comments.

Last, but not least, a special thanks to our families for their constant support—Brands, Stallcups, Hsus, and Changs; Edels, McClellands, and Moriahs. Most important, we would like to thank those closest to home. Emily, Henry, and Annabelle and Kira, Caleb, and Henry made this work possible. This book could not have been written without them. Without them, it would not have been worth writing.

The Lessons of Tragedy

Introduction

On April 4, 1968, traveling to a campaign rally in Indianapolis, Robert F. Kennedy learned that Martin Luther King Jr. had been assassinated. Kennedy took it upon himself to break the awful news to the largely African American crowd at the rally. Speaking without notes from the back of a flatbed truck, Kennedy reminded the anguished people before him that King's life had been dedicated to love and justice. It was in service of those values that King had willingly exposed himself to mortal risk. "In this difficult day, in this difficult time for the United States," Kennedy stated, "it's perhaps well to ask what kind of a nation we are and what direction we want to move in."

In answering that question he turned to the ancient Greeks. In words that might have seemed oddly detached, he told his listeners that his favorite poet was the ancient Greek tragedian Aeschylus, and reminded them that he, too, knew tragedy, having suffered the murder of a loved brother. Kennedy then recited from memory a passage from Aeschylus's play *Agamemnon:*

Even in our sleep, pain which cannot forget
Falls drop by drop upon the heart,

Until, in our own despair,
Against our will,
Comes wisdom
Through the awful grace of God.[1]

Bobby Kennedy had first encountered these ideas when Jackie Kennedy gave him her copy of Edith Hamilton's classic *The Greek Way* after John Kennedy's assassination. Hamilton's study of literature, arts, and philosophy made the point that the Greeks lived heroically. They willingly stared into the abyss of pain, despair, and disaster and somehow drew strength from those encounters. By contemplating the fragility and uncertainty of their lives, they summoned the will to act bravely, to bear the burdens of leadership, to make sacrifices in the service of great causes. In the same chapter he quoted in Indianapolis in 1968, Kennedy repeatedly underlined Hamilton's description of Aeschylus: "Life for him was an adventure, perilous indeed, but men are not made for safe havens. The fullness of life is in the hazards of life."[2] This was the message Kennedy tried to convey to an angry and distraught crowd in April 1968. Despite the nearly 2,500 years between ancient Athens and twentieth-century Indianapolis, the message of drawing inspiration from tragedy resonated.

This is not as surprising as it may sound. If there was one thing the ancient Greeks took seriously, it was tragedy. At the height of Athenian power and greatness in the fifth century BC, citizens of the world's first democracy gathered annually to experience tragedy. Great theatrical productions were staged, presented to the entire community, and supported financially by the public treasury. The subject and plot lines varied, but the form and lesson remained consistent. Prominent individuals fell from great heights due to error, ignorance, and hubris.

Societies faced disasters brought on by mistakes of commission and omission. The injunction to the Athenian citizenry was clear: the destiny of the state was in the hands of fallible men, and even in their hour of triumph great societies were perched on the precipice of catastrophe.

As Aristotle argued, this familiarity with tragedy—this tragic sensibility—entailed an understanding of "not the thing that has happened, but a kind of thing that might happen," and it was purposefully hard-wired into Athenian culture.[3] Aristotle wrote about the effect of tragedy on an audience: that they somehow liked watching the fall of the great, as it produced a feeling of horror, leading ultimately to catharsis. The catharsis was key, as tragedies not only aroused pity and fear but were intended to spur the audience into recognition that the horrifying outcomes they witnessed were eminently avoidable. By looking disaster squarely in the face, by demonstrating just how quickly things could spiral out of control, the Athenians hoped their citizenry would be charged with the sense of mutual obligation and moral courage needed to avoid such a fate.

One of the reasons people still study the classics is that they reveal timeless, elemental truths—insights about human nature and human relationships that are as applicable to our time as they were to their own. As secretary of state George Marshall remarked at the dawn of the Cold War, "I doubt seriously whether a man can think with full wisdom and with deep convictions regarding certain of the basic issues today who has not at least reviewed in his mind the period of the Peloponnesian War and the fall of Athens."[4] Indeed, the Athenians were onto something fundamental in their fascination with tragedy. For an understanding of tragedy remains indispensable—as it always has been—to the conduct of statecraft and the preservation of world order.

In every age, some of the world's leading thinkers have argued that the trajectory of humanity is a steady, even inevitable, advance toward ever-greater prosperity, peace, and moral enlightenment. In reality, the undeniable progress that humanity has made over the millennia has frequently been disrupted, even reversed, by catastrophe and collapse. In a competitive and anarchic world, the relationships between states and peoples have repeatedly been punctured by horrific breakdowns of international peace and security—veritable geopolitical cataclysms in which leading states fight for dominance and inflict appalling harm on the people caught in the crossfire. Societies are upended and even destroyed; human suffering unfolds on an epic scale; the world's most advanced nations descend into depravity; the accumulated achievements of generations crumble amid shocking violence. As the historian Donald Kagan writes, "No one can examine the grim history of the human race, repeatedly ravaged by the pain and horror of war, without feeling a great sadness at its ubiquity and perpetuity."[5] From the Peloponnesian War in the fifth century BC to the world wars of the twentieth century, the history of international affairs has often seemed a monument to tragedy.

Yet if tragedy is a curse for those who endure it, it can be a blessing for those who draw strength and wisdom from that misfortune. The memory of tragedy has often impelled the building of international orders that have succeeded—if only for a time—in holding the forces of upheaval at bay. In the wake of great geopolitical crackups, leading statesmen have found the fortitude and foresight to create new systems of norms and rules to regulate the relationships between states, and—just as critically—to erect the stable balances of power that sustain them. Driven by painful experience, they have accepted the geopolitical hardships and sacrifices necessary to avoid the far greater costs of a return to uncontrolled upheaval. Admittedly, an understanding of tragedy is not the only thing required to construct a successful international order. Yet many of the great diplomatic achievements of the modern era—the Peace of Westphalia, the Concert of Europe, and others—have rested on such an understanding. Ralph Waldo Emerson captured the basic ethos: "Great men, great nations, have not been boasters and buffoons, but perceivers of the terror of life, and have manned themselves to face it."[6]

Americans, too, once had an appreciation of tragedy. After World War II, Americans like Marshall instinctively understood—because they could so vividly remember—how terrible a rupture of world order could be, and they were constantly reminded by the looming Soviet threat that international stability could not be taken for granted. And so, over a period of decades, the United States, in cooperation with its friends and allies, undertook extraordinary geopolitical efforts to ensure that world order would not collapse once again. The result was a flawed masterpiece: a postwar international system that was never perfect but was one in which authoritarian challengers were contained and ultimately defeated, democracy and basic human rights spread more widely than ever before, and both global and American prosperity reached dizzying heights. A tragic sensibility propelled Americans to do great things.

But as has been said before, Americans are serial amnesiacs. And today, after nearly seventy-five years of great-power peace and thirty years of post–Cold War primacy, Americans are losing their sense of tragedy. The U.S.-led international order has been so successful, for so long, that Americans have come to take it for granted. They have forgotten what that order is meant to prevent in the first place: the sort of descent into violence and great-power war that has been all too common throughout human history. They are thus at risk of undermining the painstaking geopolitical exertions—the costly, frustrating, and seemingly perpetual application of American power—that have underpinned global peace and security for generations. This amnesia has become most pronounced, ironically, as U.S. power and the international order are coming under graver threat than at any time in recent memory. Revisionist states are probing aggressively for weakness; democracy is in retreat as authoritarianism again advances; instability and upheaval have reached alarming levels; the global balance of power and resolve is gradually shifting in ominous ways. The United States and the world it created are once again courting tragedy, not least because Americans are losing their ability to imagine what tragedy really is.

It does not have to be this way. The United States and its allies are not passive observers of their fate. They have the ability to counter the alarming global trends at work, so long as they can get their act together. Here history can help. A great virtue of history is that it offers vicarious experience—it provides wisdom and insight without the pain that is often the price of accumulating them. The purpose of this book is to use history to help Americans and other supporters of the U.S.-led international order rediscover their sense of tragedy *before* they have to experience it themselves. The starting point for that endeavor is an exploration of what tragedy meant to the people who invented it, more than two thousand years ago.

1

The Virtues of Tragedy

In the fifth century BC, Athens experienced a golden age. The Athenians were "addicted to innovation," a contemporary Greek observer wrote; they seemed "born into the world to take no rest themselves and to give none to others."[1] In the decades prior to the great Peloponnesian War with Sparta, that energy was on full display. The city-state of Athens—despite being a relatively small geographical entity—enjoyed the establishment of its democratic institutions, the spread of its revolutionary democratic experiment abroad, the expansion of its trade, and the ascendency of its navy. Athens emerged as an empire in its own right, leading a powerful group of allies and becoming a superpower of the ancient world. And even amid the recurring geopolitical upheavals of that era, the city saw the full flowering of its culture as it became "the school of Hellas."[2] Athenian architecture, philosophy, and literature flourished, due to some combination of restlessness, creativity, and genius, earning the Athenians a reputation for insight and innovation that persists to this day.

Nowhere was this more evident than in the rise of theatrical tragedy. "Tragedy is an achievement peculiarly Greek," the classicist Edith Hamilton wrote. "They were the first to perceive it and they lifted it to its supreme height."³ Indeed, the Athenians essentially created that art form, and they succeeded so brilliantly in developing it because they viewed it as something far greater than mere art. For the Greeks, theatrical and other dramatic representations of tragedy were public education. Tragedies were meant to serve as both a warning and a call to action. They were intended to chasten and horrify the citizenry and, in doing so, to inspire them. Athens was capable of ascending to great heights, its elites believed, but only if the public understood the depths to which it might sink absent great effort, cohesion, and courage.

I

Tragedy was a new art form in fifth-century BC Athens, but it quickly took center stage in the city's cultural, intellectual, and political life. While its exact origin remains unknown, by the early fifth century it had evolved into an annual public performance that combined choral song with spoken verse to present characters and a plot. Each spring, Athenians gathered for several days to celebrate the harvest by honoring the Greek god Dionysus. At the heart of this religious celebration, attended by as many as twenty thousand Athenians, stood the theatrical performance of tragedy.

The Athenians loved formal competitions, and the tragedies were presented as such. Assembling in the Theater of Dionysus, carved into the southern slope of the Acropolis, the Athenians listened to three different tragedians present their plays. Each playwright submitted three tragedies and a Satyr play, an irreverent take on a mythological event.

This was not only a competition, but a grand and very public one at that. The procession preceding the performances featured Athenian citizens, resident aliens, emissaries from Athens's far-flung colonies, and foreigners who had aided Athens in her efforts. It included a parade of war orphans, the conspicuous display of tributary gifts from the empire, and the brandishing of arms that underscored Athens's prowess. Attendance was subsidized, and the dramatic competition was judged by a jury of citizens chosen by lot.

Originally, the theatrical performances that accompanied this pomp revolved around song and dance, but by the fifth century BC acting, plot, and thematic resonance were the essentials of the competition. Over one thousand tragedies were produced in the fifth century alone, though only a small fraction of them have survived. Those we possess are well known: *Oedipus Rex*, *Antigone*, *The Orestia*, *The Bacchae*, and *Prometheus Bound*, among others. Yet even without all the missing plays, enough is known of the genre to suggest that it emphasized structured plots revolving around conflicts between contending, if not irreconcilable, impulses: mortals and gods; law and nature; individuals and states; order and chaos. These stories rarely ended well: the narrative arc generally culminated in the descent or destruction of a key individual, group, or society. And while tragedies often portrayed events from the mythic past, they were deliberately, if somewhat obliquely, intended to promote intense public debate about the contemporary interests and condition of the state.

Ironically enough, this point is made most clearly in a comedic rendition of a tragedy. Aristophanes composed his comedy *Frogs* in 405 BC, a year after the great tragedian Euripides had died, and at a time when the Athenian democratic experiment was in great peril. In the play, the god Dionysus decides to bring one playwright back from the underworld to save Athens. Unable to choose, he has Aeschylus and Euripides compete to determine who can make the city profit more by their instruction. Why should one admire a poet? Aeschylus asks. "Good counsel," Euripides answers, "and because we make people better members of their communities."[4] While Aristophanes' tone mocks, he captures the feeling that tragedy was a vehicle for public instruction and preservation of the city's long-term moral and political interests.

II

On the face of it, this seems strange. As Friedrich Nietzsche asked incredulously at the beginning of his philosophical inquiry *The Birth of Tragedy*, "Greeks and the pessimistic art form? The most accomplished, most beautiful, most universally envied race of mankind, those most capable of seducing us into life— they were the ones who *needed* tragedy?"[5] Why would a society at its peak choose not only to look into, but celebrate, portrayals of disaster and decline? Why would the Athenians make one of their most important civic and religious holidays about the fall of the powerful, the vicissitudes of fortune, and the meaning of sacrifice?

The short answer is because they found these performances not depressing, but inspiring. By forcing the audience to experience tragedy communally, the tragedies pushed the Greeks to grapple with their own frailty and fallibility. But by shocking, unsettling, and disturbing the audience, the tragedies also forced discussions of what was needed to circumvent such a fate. Tragedies were not, therefore, counsels of resignation or fatalism. They were calls to wisdom and action. The logic was clear enough: the Athenians saw what horrors befell their heroes, experienced pity and catharsis, arrived at new insights and were willing to make extraordinary exertions to avert the evil decree.

Often focusing on the heroic individuals of a mythic age, the Greek tragedies warned against the twin dangers of hubris and complacency. Hubris, or excessive pride, was seen as a product of past successes, overconfidence in one's infallibility, and miscalculation of one's power and capabilities. It resulted in catastrophic sins of commission—overreach, whether political or moral, and the blowback that inevitably results. The fall of Oedipus is the classic example: the arrogance, pride, and ambition of the protagonist of Sophocles' legendary play lead him first to great heights and then to his awful fate. Yet tragedies also warned that terrible traumas could result from errors of omission—from a lack of consciousness that impeded individuals and societies from preventing the eminently preventable. In both cases, tragedy represented an attempt to open viewers' eyes to impending disasters and illustrate that the Greeks' world, like the fortunes of those on the stage, was hardly as secure as it might appear. Good times, Aristotle warned, tended to produce an "arrogant and unreasonable" character.[6] This misplaced optimism lulled societies into a false sense of complacency; such complacency led to ruin.

The point of tragedy, then, was to shock the audience out of torpor. "Fear makes people inclined to deliberation," Aristotle observed in *On Rhetoric*.[7] This treatise was an extended meditation on the art of persuasion—how to move large groups through the stirring of their emotions and the appeal to reason. Here fear was a critical ingredient in concentrating the collective mind, catalyzing debate, and creating a will to act in the most difficult of circumstances. In the tragedy *Seven Against*

Thebes, for instance, Aeschylus has his heroine Antigone, steeling herself for an action that means certain death, proclaim: "Courage! The power will be mine and the means to act."[8] Or as Samuel Johnson once remarked: "Depend on it, sir, when a man knows he is to be hanged in a fortnight, it concentrates his mind wonderfully."[9]

Athenians thus dwelled on past tragedy as a way of escaping future tragedy; they used their staged performances to remind themselves of the darker possibilities lurking just below the surface of their golden age, and to find the inspiration to hold those possibilities at bay.

Reflecting on the ancient Greeks, Nietzsche observed that "we must think of the tremendous power of tragedy to excite the life of a nation, to purify and to purge."[10] The virtue of tragedy was its demand not just for clearheadedness and humility, but also for strength and communal resolve.

III

Tragedy, then, had two meanings for the Greeks. First, it referred simply to an event causing enormous suffering and destruction. Second, it referred to the *portrayal* of such catastrophes in ways meant to provoke awareness and constructive action. For the foremost Greek tragedians—Euripides, Sophocles, and Aeschylus—these twin meanings of tragedy were deeply intertwined. These writers' greatest works focused on the pitfalls that awaited even the greatest individuals, and of the inherent precariousness of even the most advanced society's achievements. This art was important for art's sake, but equally for the responses it elicited and the moral education it provided.

Aeschylus, "the father of tragedy," wove these purposes together in his classic play *The Persians,* which related how the great Persian king Xerxes had reaped the whirlwind through foolhardy foreign adventures. The play was performed in 472 BC, just eight years after the Athenians' decisive naval victory over the Persians in the battle of Salamis. It takes place in the Persian court and narrates the destruction of the Persian fleet. The Persian queen, trying to deal with her grief, summons the ghost of the former king Darius for counsel. When the ghost of Darius appears, he charges his son Xerxes with hubris for undertaking a war against the Greeks, and in particular for audaciously constructing a land bridge over the Hellespont. Shortly thereafter a bedraggled Xerxes appears on stage, lamenting the Persians' devastating reversal of fortune.

A veteran of the Persian War who had fought at Marathon and Salamis, Aeschylus dramatized the recent past to underscore the folly of overvaluing one's strengths and underestimating one's opponent. The subject would have resonated with the Athenians, because their victory over a vastly superior force—the Greek historian Herodotus counted the Persians at 1.7 million strong—had preserved the freedom of the Greeks and catapulted Athens to influence and power.[11] But this victory had come at terrible cost to the Athenians, who in the course of the war had suffered the sacking of their city and seen many of their fellow citizens perish. The Athenians who fought in this battle, many of whom would have filled the seats of the theater, had sacrificed enormously.

The play therefore works on multiple levels, lionizing the collective valor of the victorious Athenians while also evoking sympathy for the defeated Persians. And, by making the Persians sympathetic in defeat, Aeschylus suggests to his audience that they, too, could suffer overconfidence born of past victories and defeat brought on by strategic miscalculation. In a line spoken to the stage characters of the Persian court, but intended for the Athenian audience, the ghost of Darius laments that "grief is man's lot, and men must bear it. Sorrows come from sea and land; and mortal ills will multiply with mortal years."[12]

Yet it is not just the sorrow of human existence that Aeschylus addresses. The chorus asks Darius's ghost, "What conclusion shall be drawn from all that you have said?" Darius tells of his dismay with his son's multiple errors: his hubris in thinking he could subjugate all of Greece, his rashness in using all of his reserve forces, his folly in attempting to conquer nature by bridging the Hellespont and whipping the waters. The lesson is that war can unleash forces beyond the control of the state, but with dire consequences for it; dangers abound when leaders reach for objects beyond their grasp. "Dead heaped upon dead shall bear dumb witness to three generations hence that man is mortal, and must learn to curb his pride," Darius says. "All the dead are our defenders," the humbled Xerxes agrees at another point. By underestimating the risks involved in his adventures, he has left his people vulnerable.[13]

At the same time, Aeschylus offers critical insights about the sources of Athenian victory. By bringing his viewers into the inner sanctuary of their defeated enemy, Aeschylus allows the Athenians to view themselves through foreign eyes. It is notable that no individual Athenians are signaled out as particularly heroic—despite the fact that Athens triumphed—while multiple Persian warriors are referred to by name. Rather than transporting his audience to a mythic past filled with heroic actions, the play suggests that Athens's triumph was a communal victory. Through this story, Aeschylus sought to warn Athenians against the peril of strategic hubris, while also fostering the collective sacrifice and courage required to defend their society from ever-present dangers.

IV

Aeschylus, Sophocles, and Euripides were by no means uncritical supporters of the state. They judged harshly those states whose sense of justice and compassion had broken down under wartime strain, a phenomenon Athens would eventually suffer itself. Yet their works also underscored the ability to shape one's destiny through one's own choices. The tragedians repeatedly emphasized that it was only through tragedy, through unceasing struggle, that one could glimpse the heroic. Taking decisive action in the face of uncertainty and danger was critical for citizens of a democratic state assailed by forces from within and beyond their land.

Although one would hardly call these plays pro-war, themes of self-sacrifice and valiant defense of a liberal political order run throughout the known Greek tragedies. Euripides repeatedly highlighted the dignity of those individuals willing to selflessly give their lives in the protection and service of others. In the *Heracleidae*, Macaria sacrifices herself for her family. In the *Phoenician Women*, Menoiceus gives his life to save his city. In *Alcestis*, the eponymous young bride volunteers her life in exchange for her husband's.

Nowhere is the theme of individual sacrifice more prominent than in the stark tragedy *Iphigenia at Aulis*. The play centers on King Agamemnon's decision to sacrifice his daughter Iphigenia to ensure safe passage of the assembled Greek army as it deploys for the Trojan War. When Iphigenia learns that her father has lured her to Aulis in order to kill her, she grasps her father's knees and pleads for mercy. As the play reaches its climax, however, she consents to and even embraces the sacrifice to further the national cause. "My death will bring about all this liberation and my good name will live into eternity," Iphigenia declares. "People will talk about how I've saved Greece."[14]

Tragedy here took on a social and political function, as Iphigenia's stirring words were aimed directly at the Athenians sitting in the theater. "And then . . . there's also this," Iphigenia says as she contemplates her own mortality. "What right do I have to love my life so much. . . . How can I insult all those countless brave warriors and their shields, all those myriads of men, clasping hard at the oars—men with courage enough to attack our enemy and die for our country, to clear her name?"[15] Because the actor playing Iphigenia would have been a young man, entering maturity and just of age to join Athens's fights, these lines would have had double poignancy. For those about to face battle for the first time, and for those veterans and grieving widows and mothers who had known war before, the play was an effort to consecrate their struggle and validate their devotion to Athens's cause. It was also an attempt to inspire the *polis* in the face of personal and communal loss.

This points to another way that tragedy inspired its viewers to defend the free, open, and democratic order Athens had built. Euripides' *Heracleidae,* composed near the start of the Peloponnesian War, sees Demophon, the king of a mythical Athens, determined to give refugees from Argos sanctuary in his city, even if doing so risks war. To the Argive diplomat who demands the expulsion of the refugees, Demophon declares, "You won't drag these off and shame us, since we take no orders here from Argos, but we do just as we like." Because he values justice more than he fears conflict, and because the Athenians are masters of their own house, he is willing to defend the city's values with force of arms.[16]

Euripides returned to this point in *The Suppliant Women.* In this play, Theseus, the mythical founder of a democratic

Athens, intervenes in a foreign quarrel between Thebes and Argos to secure the burial of the fallen Argive warriors. In the climactic scene, a herald from Thebes—an authoritarian city-state—refuses this intervention while denigrating Athens's democracy as lacking in resolve and military capacity to enforce its will. After first defending democratic decision-making with words, Theseus resorts to its defense with arms. "If it is argument you want," Theseus tells his opponent, "this is the call of freedom."[17] Open debate was necessary to the establishment of a liberal polity, Euripides tells us, but when dealing with tyrannical foes, dialogue alone was not always sufficient for its maintenance.

Finally, these Greek dramas made the point that liberal projects grew out of intimate acquaintance with tragedy, as most famously depicted in Aeschylus's great trilogy the *Oresteia*. The trilogy, which includes the plays *Agamemnon*, *The Libation Bearers*, and *The Eumenides*, revolves around a series of killings and their aftermath: the murder of Agamemnon by his wife Clytemnestra, in revenge for his sacrifice of their daughter Iphigenia; the murder of Clytemnestra by her son Orestes, as revenge for her killing of his father; and the trial of Orestes before a jury of Athenian citizens. In the final play, *The Eumenides*, Orestes is relentlessly pursued by the Furies, three enraged goddesses of justice, until he has been acquitted in court and by the goddess Athena. At the play's conclusion, Athena convinces the Furies to accept the decision of the jury. Instead of seeking vengeance, they become honored deities in Athens who watch over the city.

The long and allegorical play concerns the epochal shift in human history away from the world of tribal blood feuds and vendettas to one of sovereign states and the rule of law. Order, represented by the state, is a deliberate step away from the violent chaos of the tribe where wrongs are avenged and perpetuated over successive generations. Subordinating oneself to the state requires accepting that its authorities possess a monopoly on the use of force in the maintenance of security and the administration of justice. Without acceptance of the state—without the willingness to defend that system internally, from society's own violent impulses, and externally, from all challenges—there is the world of disorder, chaos, and violence. Fear of falling back into such a world would spur the citizens to build the institutions and honor the norms that offered the possibility of security, stability, and justice. "What man is just that has no fear of anything?" Athena observes, noting that governing is essential to surmounting anarchy.[18] By gazing directly at such tragedies, the Greeks sought to inspire themselves to construct order out of chaos.

V

Through the experience of tragedy on the stage, the Greeks believed they could summon the strength of mind and character to avoid suffering tragedies in real life. As we will see in the next chapter, an awareness of tragedy did not allow the Greeks to stave off tragedy forever. Athens, and the Greek world more broadly, eventually succumbed to disaster on an epic scale. Yet it was that disaster that produced what is arguably the greatest tragedy to emerge from ancient Greece: Thucydides' *History of the Peloponnesian War*.

Thucydides' classic treatise is not, of course, a tragedy of the stage. Scholars have pointed to Thucydides as the first modern historian, who sought to determine the causes of contemporary events and discarded explanations that relied upon divine intervention. Yet the story he tells nonetheless represents tragedy in the grandest sense of the term.

Thucydides relates the mix of miscalculation, misfortune, and geopolitical conflict that led Athens and Sparta into a cataclysmic war, and the way that conflict distorted or simply destroyed so many of the institutions and achievements of Athens and its neighboring states. He recounts the horrors that occurred due to prolonged conflict, from enormous body counts to the erosion of democracy and human decency. He describes the way that great-power conflict caused social breakdowns that dragged much of Greece back to the tribal blood feuds that Aeschylus had portrayed on the stage. The *History of the Peloponnesian War* is a tale about the decline of a powerful empire and a whole way of life. It is rendered as artfully as any tragedy of the stage, filled with speeches, memorable leading actors, and a poetic composition that emphasizes the role of deliberate choices made by individuals in determining Athens's rise and fall.

The story thus chronicles how tragedy finally overcame the Greeks, the Athenians especially. Yet it is nonetheless cut from the same instructive cloth as many of the great tragedies of the fifth century BC. On the one hand, Thucydides emphasizes the perils of hubris and the corrosive results of extended conflict. On the other hand, his leading characters, such as the great Athenian statesman Pericles, make stirring appeals to patriotism, collective sacrifice, and perseverance in the face of danger.

Above all, Thucydides makes the point that it was when the Athenians became insufficiently attentive to tragedy that tragedy befell them. This idea is stressed in Pericles' great funeral oration. To mark the end of the first year of war, and to commemorate their dead, the Athenians hold a public burial and choose Pericles to deliver the oration. His speech is a hymn to the Athenians' character and perseverance amid great hardship. Pericles memorializes the war dead by praising what they had fought for and charging every living Athenian to "be ready to suffer in her cause."[19] What the fallen had done in their final moments—sacrificing their lives and giving the last full measure of their devotion—was precisely what ennobled them. "They joyfully determined to accept the risk" of defending their state, and in so doing accepted great individual risk in the cause of the collective good.[20] Despite the terrors of the battlefield, Pericles instructs the living to "never decline the dangers of war."[21]

But that is just what happens, as tragedy befalls Athens. In the next passage, plague descends upon the city. Thucydides lingers on the plague, describing its causes, symptoms, and effects. The plague, in his telling, marks the beginning of the end of Athenian civilization. As plague breaks loose inside Athens's walls and war rages outside of them, Thucydides describes the loosening of restraint and custom as "men now did just what they pleased. . . . Fear of gods or law of man there was none to restrain them."[22] The Athenians, wearied by their travails, seek peace with the Spartans. For all the devastation caused by the plague—scholarly estimates have placed its toll at just over a third of the Athenian population—it is this acquiescence that most angers Pericles. Rebuking his constituents, Pericles claims that "it is surely the duty of everyone to be forward in her defense." Invoking a theme that would have been familiar to the great tragedians, he instructs his audience to cease grieving "for your private afflictions, and address yourselves instead to the safety of the commonwealth."[23]

VI

Near the outset of his work, Thucydides explains that he is telling this story not simply for posterity's sake, but for the insight it can offer to those who follow.[24] By describing one monumental tragedy, Thucydides hoped to enable future leaders to avoid a similar fate. This is because Thucydides believed what so many Greek tragedians believed—that understanding the precariousness of all of humankind's achievements was essential to living wisely, living bravely, and living with purpose. A tragic sensibility may not be sufficient to ward off the dangers that threaten even the greatest societies, as the Peloponnesian War demonstrates. Yet surely it is necessary. In considering the arc of global politics over the centuries, an understanding of tragedy is equally essential.

2

Tragedy as the Norm

The ancient Greeks tried to escape tragedy by confronting it head on. Today, we try to escape tragedy by hoping it will never happen. We tend to think of a full-scale collapse of global order, an upheaval marked by cascading international instability and devastating interstate violence, as an impossibility. Great-power wars and their associated horrors are relics of a bygone era, we tell ourselves; they are scourges that afflicted earlier, less enlightened periods. But today, surely humanity and the global community have evolved sufficiently that such cataclysms will not recur; surely, as the Harvard psychologist Steven Pinker has put it, the "better angels of our nature" have subdued the demons.[1]

This belief has become particularly prominent over the past thirty years, the period since the Cold War. After the superpower contest, it often seemed that humanity had indeed reached a higher moral plane. Violent, aggressive ideologies such as communism and fascism had largely been vanquished; peaceful, positive-sum arrangements such as democracy and free markets were sweeping the globe. Europe—the crucible of great-power war for centuries—seemed thoroughly "de-bellicized," as its leading nations rapidly disarmed and pursued continental integration over geopolitical competition. Diplomatic cooperation among the leading powers in the international system was at a historic high. The forces of globalization were weaving ever-denser economic and cultural ties between nations.

Many observers glimpsed in these developments the transformation of international relations. In 1990, George H. W. Bush proclaimed a "new world order" where "the nations of the world . . . can prosper and live in harmony" and "the rule of law supplants the rule of the jungle."[2] In 2002, one of the world's leading political scientists argued that great-power war had become "literally unthinkable."[3] That same year, the administration of George W. Bush declared that "the international community has the best chance since the rise of the nation-state in the seventeenth century to build a world where great powers compete in peace instead of continually prepare for war."[4] The great challenge of the post–Cold War era, Francis Fukuyama famously predicted at the outset of that period, would not be addressing the fierce ideological competition that had previously driven the major powers to war, but would be coping with the "centuries of boredom" that would result from global peace.[5] According to this view, history would end not with a bang, but with a yawn.

Fukuyama and other heralds of the post–Cold War peace earnestly believed they were living in a brave new world. Yet they might have been chastened to know that they were singing an old song. For centuries, leading thinkers and statesmen have periodically concluded that humanity is finally leaving behind the dark shadows of geopolitical strife and entering the sunlit uplands of international harmony. They have repeatedly made the same arguments that were prominent in the heady days after the Cold War—that the moral evolution of the species was now too advanced to permit a return to the warring ways of the past, that quantum leaps in global commerce and integration were making peace too profitable to forgo, that violent ideologies were being swept aside by the forces of peace and international community. And they have repeatedly been proven wrong.

The reasons for this are relatively simple. "The sad fact," writes political scientist John Mearsheimer, "is that international politics has always been a ruthless and dangerous business, and it is likely to remain that way." States exist in a world in which there has traditionally been no "night watchman"—no supreme authority to enforce order and defend the weak.[6] The incentives for fierce, even deadly, competition are enormous, because the penalties for failing to compete effectively are so severe. The international arena is also a place in which the balance of power is constantly changing, as nations rise and decline relative to one another, and so tests of strength and competitions over status are commonplace.[7]

Not least, states are merely collections of people, motivated by fear, honor, acquisitiveness, ideology, and all the other impulses that drive humans to conflict. The result is that lasting international peace has too often proved elusive, and violent strife has been depressingly familiar. As Thomas Hobbes, the English philosopher and one of the founders of international relations realism, put it, so long as man exists in the "state of nature," so long as there is no overarching authority to provide peace and stability, human relations are destined to be characterized by "continual fear, and danger of violent death," and the "life of man" is sure to be "solitary, poor, nasty, brutish, and short."[8]

Indeed, the idea that catastrophic breakdowns of international order cannot occur in our own time betrays a very short historical memory, for such breakdowns have long represented the norm as much as the exception in global affairs. The story of international relations over the centuries has not been one of uninterrupted progress toward a kinder world. Rather, this story has been one of recurring geopolitical cataclysms in which peace is ruptured, nations are shattered, countless lives are lost or disrupted, and golden eras come crashing to an end. The specific causes and particular circumstances of these breakdowns have been multiple and varying: sometimes having to do with shifts in the balance of power, sometimes having to do with clashing ideologies, sometimes having to do with the aggressive intentions of radically revisionist powers, and sometimes having to do with the blunders, accidents, and idiosyncrasies of statecraft. But their ferocity, scale, and escalation have almost always taken contemporaries by surprise, and their consequences have often been horrific. In an anarchic world characterized by high-stakes competition, tragedy is a fact of international life. After all, it happened to the Greeks.

I

The Athenians were second to none in their efforts to cultivate a tragic sensibility. Yet tragedy nonetheless struck in the fifth century BC, when Athens and Sparta came to blows in the great Peloponnesian War. The war was not entirely unforeseen, as tensions between the two superpowers of ancient Greece had been rising for years. But the timing and rapidity of its outbreak were. Some fifty years earlier, Sparta and Athens had cooperated to defeat a Persian invasion, thereby saving Greece from foreign domination and ushering in an era of Greek power and prominence on the world stage. And despite fighting one inconclusive conflict from 460 BC to 445 BC, the two Greek rivals had more recently undertaken a revolutionary effort to preserve the peace. They signed what was then a highly innovative peace settlement that committed the parties to respect each other's spheres of influence and to settle disputes through arbitration. The truce held for nearly fifteen years, but in 431 BC the Athenians and Spartans again took up arms.

As so often with great wars, the precipitating causes were seemingly trivial—disputes among allies of the two ancient superpowers, Athenian economic sanctions against a city-state allied with Sparta, quarrels involving locales so obscure that Thucydides later had to remind his readers where some of them were. Yet according to Thucydides, the underlying, true causes of the war were timeless and profound. Over the years leading up to the fighting, the Spartans had viewed the rise of an Athenian empire as a growing challenge to Sparta's primacy among the Greek city-states. The ideological cleavages between a democratic, commercially minded Athens—the Greek world's leading sea power—and a militarized, slave-holding Sparta—the era's leading land power—stoked the tensions. As hostilities threatened, concerns about national honor, credibility, and economic security exacerbated pressures for war. When the match was finally thrown, both sides believed—in a textbook illustration of miscalculation fueled by overconfidence—that the conflict would play to their respective strengths, and that it would be short, limited, and triumphant. Both soon came to realize that the fire, once started, was not so easily contained.[9]

The Peloponnesian War was a classic case in which two enemies possessing very different forms of power inflicted severe pain on each other, but neither could achieve—for many years, at least—a knockout blow. Meanwhile, the bipolar structure of Greek geopolitics ensured that the fighting spiraled into what must have seemed like a world war, as allies, neutrals, and most of the known world were pulled into the vortex of a conflict that lasted nearly three decades. As the struggle intensified, the stakes grew progressively higher, and both sides found themselves ruled by their most demagogic and hawkish factions. "The whole Hellenic world was convulsed," Thucydides wrote. "There was nothing on a greater scale, either in war or in other matters."[10]

The consequences were certainly far beyond what either side had initially imagined. Greece had been enjoying an age of great achievement and creativity in the decades prior to the conflict. Athens in particular was at the height of its economic prosperity and cultural sophistication, and its liberal constitution was a model for other Greek city-states aspiring to democracy. It was the time of Sophocles, Aeschylus, Socrates, Thucydides, and Hippocrates. Yet so much of this progress collapsed under the pressure of prolonged war.

"Never had so many cities been taken and laid desolate," Thucydides recorded; "never was there so much banishing and bloodshedding."[11] The fighting inflicted appalling economic damage on both sides, by halting trade, destroying crops, and disrupting the normal patterns of cultivation and commerce. The human costs were even worse, as some city-states lost nearly their entire male populations to violence, hunger, and disease. Moreover, the war fundamentally changed both Athenian and Spartan society, degrading their political institutions, causing breakdowns of social order, unleashing widespread communal violence, and eroding long-held views of morality and justice. Ethnic cleansing, torture and execution of prisoners, and abuse and enslavement of noncombatants became common; norms regarding treatment of enemies and fellow citizens were progressively cast aside.

Thucydides' most memorable passages deal with the moral and social breakdowns that flowed from geopolitical upheaval. As the war spreads and its ideological overtones grow, the citizens of Corcyra, divided by the war into pro-Athens and pro-Sparta factions, "engaged in butchering those of their fellow-citizens whom they regarded as their [political] enemies." "Death thus raged in every shape," Thucydides writes; "and as usually happens at such times, there was no length to which violence did not go; sons were killed by their fathers, and supplicants dragged from the altar or slain upon it."[12] The basis of human civilization breaks down under this stress, as family relations surrender to partisan bloodletting.

Most notoriously, in the Melian Dialogue, the Athenians demonstrate the war's coarsening effect on their sense of basic decency. They demand that Melos, a neutral island in the Aegean, pay tribute to Athens. When the Melians appeal for mercy, the Athenians coldly inform them that "the strong do what they can and the weak suffer what they must." To prove the point, they systematically murder the Melian men and sell the women and children into slavery. War "proves a rough master," Thucydides observes, stripping away rationality and humanity, and replacing them with something darker, more passionate, and less susceptible to restraint.[13]

In the end, the Spartans defeated Athens, tearing down its famed long walls, destroying its fleets, and reasserting their primacy within the Greek world. Yet the Peloponnesian War proved so costly in lives and treasure that it devastated winner and loser alike. The Greek city-states emerged from the war divided, morally degraded, and vulnerable to foreign intervention and conquest; the conflict would ultimately lead to the eclipse of the Greeks as powerful and independent actors on the world stage. Thucydides immodestly claimed that his history would serve as a "possession for all time."[14] The Peloponnesian War offers a timeless reminder that the potential for tragedy continually stalks human affairs.

II

It is tempting to think that this is just ancient history—that the fall into depravity Thucydides describes was the peculiar province of an era vastly different from our own. Unfortunately, more recent history gives little reason to think that the underlying logic of global affairs has changed. Just consider the record of European geopolitics.

For nearly five hundred years prior to the mid-twentieth century, Europe stood at the center of the international system. Throughout this period, Europe was known as much for the ubiquity of its violence as for its economic, technological, and cultural achievements. Many of the continent's major powers were at war more often than they were at peace. By one count, Russia experienced only a single quarter-century of peace during the thousand-year period from 900 to 1900. England, over a similar period, was involved in some type of war during fifty-six out of every one hundred years.[15] "Peace," writes the military historian Michael Howard, was "regarded as a brief interval between wars. . . . War . . . remained an almost automatic activity, part of the natural order of things."[16] And even when European societies were at the peak of their sophistication and dominance, the continent suffered repeated descents into disaster. Each of these conflagrations was preceded by sharpening challenges to, and then surprisingly precipitous breakdowns of, the prevailing international order. In each case, the ensuing destruction was appalling.

Start with the Thirty Years' War, which raged from 1618 to 1648. That conflict represented the climax of a period of escalating religious tensions unleashed by the Protestant Reformation, as well as the culmination of a struggle by Europe's great powers for influence within the weak and fragmented Holy Roman Empire. In retrospect, it seems obvious that an explosion was inevitable, in view of the increasingly incendiary manner in which religious and geopolitical tensions were interacting with one another prior to the conflict. Throughout the empire, governments were augmenting their arsenals and bolstering their fortifications; religious splits were widening; hardliners were gaining the ascendancy. Yet as with the Peloponnesian War, the speed and totality of the coming crackup were far from universally foreseen. Just a year before the war broke out, in fact, many of Europe's ongoing conflicts seemed to be de-escalating. One English diplomat declared that war was receding and that "calm and Halcyonian days" were in store for "the greatest part of Christendome."[17]

The conflict did come, of course, the triggers—which seem hopelessly obscure today—being a succession crisis in Bohemia and the defenestration of Catholic dignitaries by Protestant firebrands in Prague. When it did, the interlocking nature of Europe's conflicts ensured that it spiraled out of control. Nearly all the continental powers were drawn into the struggle, sometimes reluctantly and sometimes enthusiastically, sometimes for religious reasons and sometimes for geopolitical motives, sometimes in bids for aggrandizement and sometimes to prevent a feared rival from profiting. The fighting spread as far as Portugal; it drew in countries from Spain and France to Sweden and Denmark.

The addition of new combatants, in turn, prolonged the war by providing fresh armies and making any potential peace settlement ever more complex; the interweaving of political and religious issues further obstructed a resolution by making compromise with "enemies of God" seem tantamount to theological treason. What began as a civil war between factions in the Holy Roman Empire became a conflict in which those parties were essentially at the mercy of the more powerful outside actors that had subsequently joined the fray. "I am very much afraid that the states of the Empire, quarreling fiercely among themselves, may start a fatal conflagration embracing not only themselves . . . but also all those countries that are in one way or another connected with Germany," one observer had predicted in 1615. "All this will undoubtedly produce the most dangerous consequences."[18]

"Dangerous" doesn't describe the half of it. Within the Holy Roman Empire, the war caused demographic disaster—a population decline of between 15 and 33 percent even by fairly conservative estimates, equivalent to some 48 to 105 million American deaths today.[19] Entire areas were effectively depopulated; destruction of livestock and crops, pillaging of wealth and resources, and other disruptions sent an already feeble economy into free fall. Political order and existing social structures broke down in areas where the fighting raged; in the resulting vacuums, all manner of atrocities, even cannibalism, occurred. The war was, quite simply, hellish for people on the path of the armies that marched through, as religious hatreds combined with the passions inevitably unleashed by conflict to cause a slide into barbarism.

The sacking of the Protestant city of Magdeburg by Catholic armies in 1631 was uniquely awful. The city was burned to the ground and twenty thousand of its inhabitants were butchered. It was an episode, one survivor later wrote, "which cannot be adequately described with words or sufficiently lamented with tears."[20] But if Magdeburg was the Corcyra of the Thirty Years' War, rape, torture, murder, deprivation, and countless other forms of mistreatment were everyday affairs in a three-decade struggle that unleashed the religious and geopolitical furies of a continent. "Every soldier needs three peasants," went one contemporary saying: "One to give up his lodgings, one to provide his wife, and one to take his place in Hell."[21]

III

The carnage of the Thirty Years' War eventually ended with the Peace of Westphalia.[22] Those accords hardly reduced the frequency of great-power conflicts in the following decades, although they did significantly lessen their intensity. The European powers fought forty-eight wars between 1648 and 1789, with some of them—the War of the Spanish Succession from 1701 to 1714 and the Seven Years' War from 1756 to 1763— amounting to world wars in all but name.[23] Yet Westphalia did at least drain these struggles of their religious content and generally made them less devastating in their effects. Wars were primarily fought by relatively small, professional armies; the aims of the combatants were more often limited than total. By the mid- to late eighteenth century, there were renewed hopes that Europe might be conquering the scourge of war altogether.

Enlightenment thinkers argued that denser ties of investment and trade were transforming international relations and making bellicosity too costly to contemplate. "Wherever there is commerce," wrote Montesquieu in 1748, "there are soft manners and morals."[24] New or improved forms of communication, such as newspapers and epistolary novels, were raising European consciousness of what would today be called human rights and fostering a nascent international community opposed to conquest and aggression. In some quarters, the French Revolution and toppling of the Bourbon monarchy even raised hopes that aggressive despotisms were giving way to more pacific governments of the people. In 1795, Immanuel Kant published his famous essay "Perpetual Peace," arguing that the spread of democracy, international organizations, and a sense of "world citizenship" could allow mankind to banish the blight of war.[25] Yet it was not only philosophers who were optimistic about the future. "Unquestionably," William Pitt the Younger, one of Britain's greatest prime ministers, told the House of Commons in 1792, "there was never a time in the history of this country when, from the situation in Europe, we might more reasonably expect fifteen years of peace, than we may at the present moment."[26]

Pitt's foresight could not have been worse. In nearly every era, revolutions within states touch off conflicts between them, by upsetting established power dynamics and unleashing new and often aggressive ideologies. Hardly had Pitt spoken, in fact, when the wars of the French Revolution began. The French Revolution turbocharged traditional French nationalism by infusing it with a messianic ideological impulse. Paris now sought to export its revolution through a "crusade for universal liberty," while Europe's conservative monarchies—terrified of political contagion and hoping to carve off pieces of France for themselves—endeavored to strangle the revolutionary baby in its cradle.[27] What started with a French invasion of the Austrian Netherlands in 1792 turned into a generation of conflict that would not subside until Napoleon's final overthrow in 1815.

The defining features of those conflicts, like the Thirty Years' War before them, were how widely they spread and how all-encompassing they became. With France assaulting the continental balance of power and the political stability of nearly all its neighbors, the wars soon drew in every major country in Europe. As French conquests accumulated and

French ambitions grew, the fighting would ultimately rage as far afield as the Caribbean and the Middle East. The geographic expansion of these conflicts, in turn, was both equaled by and related to their intensity. The French were fighting not for limited aims but to dominate the European landscape; the European monarchies were fighting not just to subdue France but to extinguish the flame of revolution. It was "a war to the death," wrote one Frenchman, "which we will fight . . . so as to destroy and annihilate all who attack us, or to be destroyed ourselves."[28]

Indeed, the historian David Bell calls the struggles that followed the French Revolution the "first total war," because of the ferocity of the fighting, the totality of the aims, and the unprecedented mobilization of the masses. The French used the *levée en masse* and the ideological nature of the conflicts to tap the energies of the nation writ large; France's opponents continually intensified their own exertions in response. The size of battles and armies increased several times over; the fighting continued despite losses that earlier would have been crippling. "Before 1790," notes Bell, "only a handful of battles had involved more than 100,000 combatants"; in 1813, "the battle of Leipzig drew 500,000, with fully 150,000 of them killed or wounded."[29] "There seemed no end to the resources mobilized," the Prussian soldier and military theorist Carl von Clausewitz, who had witnessed the Napoleonic onslaught firsthand, later wrote; "all limits disappeared in the vigor and enthusiasm shown by governments and their subjects. . . . War, untrammeled by any conventional restrains, had broken loose in all its elemental fury."[30]

For those who experienced it, the fury was profound. Nearly every country on the continent experienced changes in its frontiers or political system. The global economy was wrenched by blockades and scorched-earth campaigns; conventional warfare and guerrilla struggles inflicted shocking

levels of devastation from Portugal to Russia. The human suffering was vast, with perhaps seven million soldiers and civilians
killed between 1792 and 1815.[31] And as invariably occurs in such
conflicts, morality, justice, and human decency were among the
first casualties. "It has cost us dearly to return . . . to the principles that characterized the barbarism of the early ages of
nations," Napoleon acknowledged, "but we have been constrained . . . to deploy against the common enemy the arms he
has used against us."[32] The wars of the French Revolution were
not just a geopolitical disruption; they brought the seeming
moral progress of the Enlightenment screeching to a halt.

IV

The experience was so searing that the remaining great powers
resolved, after Napoleon's eventual defeat, to ensure that such
tragedies would never be permitted to recur. And for roughly
one hundred years, Europe did manage to avert another all-out
crack-up. Humanity's irrepressible optimism reasserted itself;
it was common to hear in the late nineteenth and early twentieth centuries that a new day of peace and harmony was dawning. The British author Norman Angell would immortalize
himself by suggesting, just a few years before World War I, that
what we would now call globalization had rendered great-
power conflict obsolete.[33] Yet if Angell's timing was exquisitely
bad, he had good company in the multitude of thinkers who
believed that improved communications were knitting humanity ever more tightly together, that international arbitration was
making war unnecessary, and that nationalism was being suppressed by newer, more enlightened ideologies.

"The preservation of a general peace and a possible reduc-
tion in the excessive armaments that now burden every nation

are ideals towards which all governments should strive," Czar
Nicholas II of Russia declared in 1898.[34] The years after the czar's
appeal were a time of international conferences devoted to
promoting the cause of peace. Treaties limiting the use of in-
humane weapons and tactics proliferated. Europe as a whole
was more peaceful than it had ever been before, with not just
interstate warfare but violence of all kinds in sharp decline.
Optimism that war could be controlled if not eliminated was
probably more widespread than in any previous era.

How quickly and painfully these hopes came crashing
down. Even amid the optimism of the late Victorian era, a variety of deep geopolitical and ideological trends were setting
the stage not for a new era of peace but for a return to great-
power war. Dangerous shifts in the balance of power, instability caused by the weakening of the Austro-Hungarian and
Ottoman Empires, the rigidities created by opposing alliance
systems and hair-trigger military plans, the rise of social Dar-
winist and militarist ideas that exalted the role of war in human
and national development, the tensions surrounding Germany's
bid for European preeminence and world power—these developments created the great mass of combustible material that
was set off by a seemingly minor spark, the assassination of the
archduke Franz Ferdinand, in the summer of 1914.

The resulting war was a conflict that none of the key actors
truly wanted—even the most aggressive, Germany, preferred a
short, localized war in the Balkans, rather than the all-
consuming maelstrom that occurred—and one that most
people imagined could be avoided or contained until the very
eve of war. And even as the great nations of Europe slid over
the precipice, all imagined that the fighting would be brief and
glorious. Instead, what Theodore Roosevelt called "that great
black tornado" swept up everything in its path.[35] The prolifera-

tion of trench networks on the Western front in late 1914 and
after was an apt metaphor for a conflict that sprawled into
Africa, the Middle East, and East Asia, that sucked in nations
from Japan to the United States, and that turned a globalized
age into a globalized war.

World War I dealt a staggering blow to the notion of historical progress, as it demonstrated that the more advanced
societies became, the more devastating the collisions between
them could be. In September 1914, the *Economist* had assured
its readers of "the economic and financial impossibility of car-
rying out hostilities many more months on the present scale."[36]
Yet in reality, the development of more capable states provided
Europe's rulers with the ability to tax and conscript their populations and otherwise sustain a catastrophic conflict longer than
anyone might have imagined; the industrial and technological
breakthroughs of the age now allowed killing on an industrial
scale. In the end, the war would produce a butcher's bill of
perhaps fifteen million soldiers and civilians killed. Meanwhile,
mankind crossed new frontiers of destruction as prior ethical
prohibitions eroded and innovations such as aerial bombing,
poison gas, and unrestricted submarine warfare were intro-
duced; the war precipitated the genocide of the Armenians and
countless other crimes against noncombatants. "The horrors of
war in ancient times would be nothing compared with the horrors of war today," the rector of one British church observed.
"All the resources of science had been called upon to perfect
weapons of destruction for mankind."[37]

The long-term consequences were equally traumatic.
World War I and its aftermath toppled empires, remade the
political map of continents, and set off revolutions from the
heart of Europe to the Far East. It led to the rise of a new generation of leaders, in some of the foremost industrial societies

of the world, who glorified rather than abhorred organized violence, and it incubated some of the most poisonous political ideologies—communism and fascism—in human history. "For us," explained one Italian fascist, "the war has never come to an end. We simply replaced external enemies with internal ones."[38] World War I was "the deluge . . . a convulsion of nature," remarked Britain's David Lloyd George, "an earthquake which is upheaving the very rocks of European life."[39]

Those who suffered through World War I could at least take comfort in the fact that it was meant to be "the war to end all wars." Yet the sacrifices of the Great War ultimately purchased only twenty years' respite before the eruption of an even greater war. In retrospect, it is easy to trace the origins of World War II—in the flawed peace settlement that left Germany permanently aggrieved but not permanently subdued, in the Great Depression and the stimulus it provided to political and geopolitical radicalism, in the radically predatory ideologies and foreign policies of the revisionist powers, namely Japan and Nazi Germany.[40] To borrow from Leon Trotsky, status-quo powers such as Great Britain, France, and the United States may not have been interested in great-power war in the aftermath of World War I, but the aggressive worldviews and ambitions of leaders in Tokyo, Berlin, and Rome ensured that great-power war was still interested in them. Yet in this prewar period as in so many others, even the most hard-headed observers found it difficult to grasp the scale and imminence of what was coming.

Winston Churchill would later be lionized for sensing the gravity of the threat before his contemporaries, but in the late 1920s he contemptuously rejected naval rearmament on grounds that "no naval war against a first class Navy is likely to take place in the next twenty years."[41] For others, the failure of imagination was far worse. In 1928, statesmen of most of the world's leading nations solemnly signed the Kellogg-Briand Pact, which renounced aggression as a tool of state policy. In 1931, a mere eight days before Japan's invasion of Manchuria, Britain's Lord Cecil assured the League of Nations that "there has scarcely ever been a time in the world's history when war seems less likely than it does at present."[42] As late as 1938, Britain's Neville Chamberlain could promise that handing over the Sudetenland to Hitler would bring "peace for our time."[43] If the civilized world was slow to react to Hitler's rise, it was precisely because so many leading thinkers and statesmen could hardly conceive of how fully and catastrophically the system was about to break once again. The major democracies, writes historian James Sheehan, neglected their "security needs after 1919, in part because ordinary people, as well as their leaders, could not bring themselves to believe that anyone would be foolish enough to inflict another major war on Europe."[44]

When the break did occur, it dwarfed the effects of those that had preceded it. Nations struggled not simply for advantage or territory but for survival; over sixty million people died in a conflict that fused hyper-charged strategic competition to some of the most toxic racialized ideologies ever seen. For populations from the Atlantic to Southeast Asia, the war was not some abstract geopolitical chess match. It was an intensely tangible catastrophe that took the form of rape and torture, starvation and disease, genocide and ethnic cleansing, deprivation and economic collapse, and death in all its varied forms. Even more so than earlier conflicts, the war swept away prior moral considerations, unleashing practices from the terror bombing of civilians to the attempted extermination of entire religious and ethnic groups.

Without a doubt, the Axis powers were by far the greatest offenders in this regard. Yet even the Western democracies were drawn into the same downward spiral of depravity; even they eventually came to deliberately target civilians in an effort to undermine their will to fight. As British prime minister Stanley Baldwin had predicted, "You would have to kill more civilians, more women and children, first, if you want to save yours from the enemy."[45] The war finally ended in 1945, with the use of atomic weapons that themselves set new standards for indiscriminate destruction, and yet were still seen, rightly, as the best way to bring the fighting to a close.[46] By that point, Europe's time atop global politics had come to an end—and much of Eurasia was a devastated hell-scape and a monument to what happens when international order gives way.

V

When we assume that the arc of human events bends inevitably toward a better world, we forget that the trajectory of global affairs has too frequently ended in tragedy. Breakdowns of international peace and security are not anomalies or anachronisms; they veritably litter the historical landscape. And whatever their proximate causes and particularities, the common theme is that they have often unfolded with a pace, intensity, ferocity, and scope that have stunned even the sharpest minds of the day. "Every war is ironic," writes Paul Fussell, "because every war is worse than expected."[47] The bad news is therefore that there is something inherently tragic about world politics—in international affairs as in Greek drama, disaster is never far away. The good news is that tragedy has also provided inspiration for those who have periodically tried, and sometimes even succeeded, to steer history onto a better path.

3
Tragedy as Inspiration

Plato said that funeral speeches are meant to advise the living by praising the dead.[1] Taking the stage on the town common in Keene, New Hampshire, in 1884, Oliver Wendell Holmes Jr., shortly to become one of America's most famous jurists, gave perhaps the most famous Memorial Day speech in American history. "We are in the presence of the dead," he declared. Memorializing his fallen comrades from the Civil War, Holmes recalled that "in our youth our hearts were touched with fire. It was given to us to learn at the outset that life is a profound and passionate thing." And in praising his own generation's courage in the face of death, Holmes drew inspiration to act in the present. "As I listen," he said, "the great chorus of life and joy begins again, and amid the awful orchestra of seen and unseen powers and destinies of good and evil our trumpets sound once more a note of daring, hope, and will."[2] Here was the lesson of Greek tragedy: by connecting with a tragic past, individuals could find the courage to strive in the face of an unknown future.

In international relations, too, death and trauma can be sources of inspiration. The history of international relations

often seems a tale of unyielding woe. Yet memory of past catastrophic upheavals has, on multiple occasions, played a more
constructive role by catalyzing creative diplomacy meant to
prevent or at least delay their repetition. "The great moments
of international order building have tended to come after major wars," G. John Ikenberry observes, because such wars sweep
away the old order and create the imperative to build a new one
in its place.[3]

In its simplest form, an international order is the system
of rules, norms, and power relationships that regulates international affairs. Order-building projects thus represent deliberate efforts, undertaken by the world's leading nation or nations,
to escape Hobbes's state of nature and create some measure
of structure and stability in an anarchical world. Durable international orders rest on more than historical memory, of
course: they are also critically dependent on favorable balances
of power and a commitment to shared values. Yet as Holmes
would have understood, the recollection of tragedy has often
motivated states and leaders to summon their power in the
service of order. When successful, those orders have held
back or at least mitigated the forces of destruction—if only for
a while.

                                    I

All these things were true of the project that established the
modern international system of sovereign nation-states. Following the shattering violence of the Thirty Years' War, the
rulers of Europe signed the Peace of Westphalia in 1648. That
peace, which resulted from protracted negotiations involving
over one hundred parties, and which consisted of not one but
multiple treaties signed over the course of the year, covered an

array of issues and grievances, and drew on a variety of diplomatic and legal precedents established in the prior century. Yet the cumulative result was a diplomatic revolution. Westphalia sought to tame Europe's confessional conflicts by establishing norms against interference in other states' domestic affairs, making secular rather than religious authority the basis for state sovereignty, and checking aggression through the maintenance of a balance of power rather than appeals to universal morality. The architects of Westphalia aimed to create a system that could limit, if not extinguish, the religious passions and geopolitical ambitions that had recently ravaged Europe. The measure of their success was that it would be over 140 years until the continent's next great collapse.

The Westphalian breakthrough hardly came about naturally, for the same conflicts and zealotry that brought on the Thirty Years' War had long impeded its resolution. "I would rather die than grant any concessions to the sectarians when it comes to religion," Ferdinand II, the Holy Roman Emperor who did much to ignite and perpetuate the conflict, had once said.[4] What ultimately opened the way to a settlement, then, was not some revolutionary moral advance. It was a combination of military exhaustion and the dawning recognition that some new system was needed to prevent Europe from bleeding itself white once again. Having marched across Germany during the war, a Swedish general later recalled, "I would not have believed a land could have been so despoiled had I not seen it with my own eyes."[5] The central intellectual pillar of Westphalia was the widespread conviction that such a cataclysm must not recur. "Since the grievances of the one and the other religion . . . have been for the most part the cause and occasion of the present war," one of the key Westphalian treaties explained, defusing those grievances must be at the heart of the settlement.[6]

Indeed, a principal reason the negotiations were so tortuous—they lasted, in one form or another, for half a decade—is that they involved more than merely disentangling the contending parties within the Holy Roman Empire and across Europe as a whole. The diplomats also had to create a new framework for how peoples, leaders, and states would relate to one another. "As far as the peace talks are concerned," the Swedish chancellor Count Axel Oxenstierna wrote to his son, the head of the Swedish delegation, "do not let yourself be disturbed that they go so slowly.... Powerful and cunning enemies, ill-willed allies, the interests of all the powers and republics of Europe struggling with each other can make a confusing negotiation and disguise the outcome . . . but . . . great negotiations require a long time and great men."[7] The eventual result was a set of agreements that brought the Thirty Years' War to a close, while also restraining the impulse to universalism and thereby bounding the severity and duration of future conflicts.

The parties accepted the principle of *cuius regio, euius religio,* under which the rulers of the constituent parts of the empire were free to choose the established religion of their own states. Crucially, however, those rulers were also required to grant Protestants and Catholics alike freedom of worship. Ferdinand II might have preferred to perish rather than concede such a heresy, and the Holy See denounced the accord as "null, void, invalid, iniquitous, unjust, damnable, reprobate, inane, empty of meaning and effect for all time."[8] Yet the key achievement of Westphalia—enabled, as it happened, by the death or removal of Ferdinand II and other intransigent leaders—was precisely in recognizing while also limiting the religious authority of rulers. In the same vein, Westphalia enshrined the principle of state sovereignty. By acknowledging the exclusive authority of each state over its own territory and citizens, the agreements created a set of norms designed to strengthen the power of rulers within their own frontiers while restraining—if hardly eliminating—their propensity to meddle abroad.

Accompanying these innovations was a new diplomatic and legal architecture designed to discourage war before it started and control its furies once it had begun. The Dutch jurist Hugo Grotius laid the conceptual groundwork in his work *The Law of War and Peace,* published as the conflict raged. "Throughout the Christian world," Grotius wrote, "I have seen a lawlessness in warfare that even barbarian races would think shameful." War without restraint destroyed the basis for society and civilization. It was thus necessary "to assuage, as far as I could, that savagery . . . in making and waging war" by specifying the circumstances in which use of force was justified, outlining a code of conduct to which all warring parties should be bound, and—most ambitiously—advancing the idea of a "common law between nations," or a concept of international society in which all members agreed to honor and enforce certain basic rules.[9] Westphalia, with its emphasis on respect for sovereignty and limits, was the diplomatic realization of this intellectual effort. Building on older precedents, Westphalia also established other diplomatic customs—permanently stationing diplomatic representatives in foreign capitals, convening international summits and consultations—in hope of regulating relations and settling disputes.[10]

Treaties and norms alone could not maintain the peace, however, and so the geopolitical underpinning of all this innovation was a deliberate emphasis on maintaining a stable balance of power—one that would prevent any state from overturning the European order or touching off another all-consuming conflagration. During the Thirty Years' War, France's Cardinal Richelieu had established himself as a pioneer of

European raison d'état. He had worked assiduously to prevent consolidation of a unified central Europe that would have been strong enough to threaten France, even though this meant forsaking the principle of religious solidarity with the empire's Catholic rulers. "The state has no immortality," he decreed, "its salvation is now or never."[11]

After Westphalia, this search for equilibrium—as opposed to heavenly salvation—became the primary preoccupation of most European princes. When France, now driven by the ambitions of the self-professed "Sun King," Louis XIV, made multiple bids for continental primacy, the result was not French dominance but successful balancing by an ever-shifting coalition of states. To those who argued that pursuing such a policy required a cold-blooded, occasionally amoral realpolitik, the response might have been that this was far better than a return to hot-blooded religious fanaticism. "Reason of state is a wonderful beast," remarked one astute observer following the Westphalian congress, "for it chases away all other reasons."[12]

As always, the burdens of equilibrium were heavy. England, which organized the key balancing coalitions, was involved in repeated crises, conflicts, and wars with France over much of the late seventeenth and eighteenth centuries. Public debt exploded from three million pounds in the 1680s, to 100 million by 1760, to 300 million in 1796, to 745 million in 1815, as London funded a powerful navy and subsidized continental allies that could threaten France and resist its ambitions.[13] These exertions were tremendously expensive, but to England's leaders, they still seemed much cheaper than the potential costs of not making them.

The payoff was that, in the generations after 1648, Westphalia and the policies that supported it sustained a precarious equilibrium in Europe. The threat of conflict was usually high, and dozens of wars occurred as the balance was tested and re-inforced. Yet through the 1780s, the European order never simply collapsed as it had during the Thirty Years' War. The Holy Roman Empire went from being "the disaster zone of Europe" to a loose but fairly stable confederation of largely autonomous states; confessional politics and creedal passions receded from European geopolitics.[14] When Europe's rulers did go to war, the principles enshrined in Westphalia ensured that their objectives tended to be comparatively limited—rarely did states seek the utter destruction and extermination of their enemies—and the conduct of their armies comparatively restrained.[15] All this represented an imperfect achievement. Yet it was a marked improvement upon the catastrophe that had preceded and inspired it.

II

That achievement would last only until the French Revolution ravaged the European landscape by letting loose a new messianic ideology and a new approach to mobilizing societies for conquest. In the wake of the ensuing quarter-century of conflict, however, there emerged the Concert of Europe, alternatively known as the Congress system. This order, which had visionary statesmen Viscount Castlereagh of Britain, Klemens von Metternich of Austria, and Charles Maurice de Talleyrand of France among its founders, was designed to prevent Europe from once again sliding into interminable warfare and ideological conflict. Its success was arguably more complete, if not quite as long-lasting, as that of the Westphalian order. On the heels of a series of wars that often seemed unlimited in both their aims and their harsh effects, Europe would, over the course of roughly a century, make greater strides toward peace and stability than in any prior era.

The former led directly to the latter: the Concert of Europe was suffused with a tragic sensibility fostered by the traumas associated with the French Revolution. The existential struggles between the continent's greatest powers, the revolutionary social and political changes wrought by invasion and conflict, the vast human suffering and economic destruction, and the diplomatic disputes that had repeatedly allowed Napoleon to divide and defeat the powers opposing him all combined to create a new moment of intellectual clarity—a consensus among Europe's leading statesmen that extraordinary measures were required to prevent the forces of chaos from being unchained again. Defeating Napoleon was but the first task, wrote Castlereagh in 1815. The larger issue was that of "securing that repose which all the Powers of Europe so much require."[16] Czar Alexander of Russia agreed: "The course *formerly* adopted by the Powers in their mutual relations had to be *fundamentally* changed."[17]

The Concert achieved this goal by drawing the major European powers into an order prejudiced toward stability, moderation, and peace. That order rested, in part, on the conservative political values and abhorrence of revolution that prevailed in most European capitals after the Napoleonic era, which provided a crucial degree of ideological cohesion. It rested on the redrawing of Europe's political map that occurred as the Napoleonic wars came to a close, in a way that settled territorial disputes and provided security buffers between powerful states. Most fundamentally, the system rested on the geopolitical commitment of Europe's major powers.

The victors of the Napoleonic wars—Austria, Great Britain, Prussia, and Russia—bound themselves together in the Quadruple Alliance, dedicated to defeating any resurgence of French aggression. Russia and Britain, the most powerful of the victors, anchored the order through their willingness to put down any significant challenge to the European balance.[18] Yet these measures were coupled with the preservation of France as a relatively strong and unified political entity, and with a commitment to allow that country—which had just recently rampaged across the European world—to rejoin the system at an early moment, as it did in 1818. The goal of the postwar settlement was thus not vengeance or ostracism, but equilibrium. France was to be both restrained by and integrated into a structure that gave all the major powers a stake in its success.

Critically, that structure was also reinforced by a commitment to shared practices and norms. The creators of the Concert never imagined, as some later statesmen did, that it would be possible to fully transcend the conflicting interests between states. They did, however, understand that the unconstrained, Hobbesian pursuit of near-term unilateral advantage was unlikely to produce a lasting peace. Europe's equilibrium, wrote Metternich, "can only last so long as certain large States are animated by a spirit of moderation and justice which will preserve that equilibrium."[19] So these leaders created formal mechanisms and understandings designed to manage the inevitable crises and preserve a broader "system," as Castlereagh phrased it, that would be "best for the general interest."[20]

To that end, the Concert entailed an explicit understanding that the major powers of Europe had a special responsibility to preserve the peace—to discourage revolutionary upheavals and maintain the continental status quo. Those powers agreed to treat the territorial settlement that followed the war as a unified whole that must not be violated, even in part—no unilateral territorial changes would be tolerated. Not least, the Concert institutionalized high-level diplomatic conferences as a way of channeling disputes into the diplomatic and legal realms and coordinating action when necessary. To an even greater degree than after Westphalia, peacetime crisis management now become the regular preoccupation of Europe's leading states. Metternich believed, with some justification, that this entire system represented a historical breakthrough: "No great political insight is needed to see that this Congress could not be modeled on any which had taken place."[21]

Collectively, then, the authors of the Concert system were not entirely cynical, but neither were they naïve. They audaciously sought to build an innovative structure of peace, one that would temper the competitive impulses that had previously driven Europe to destruction. Yet they also understood that human nature had not changed—that even the most elegant diplomatic processes would work only if supported by a balance of power that encouraged restraint and penalized aggression. "To keep France in order," Castlereagh observed, "we require great masses. . . . Prussia, Austria, and Russia ought to be as great and powerful as they have ever been."[22] In the same way, the system would endure only if the keepers of the peace were ready to spring into action when threats emerged and the key principles of the settlement were challenged—which Britain and Russia repeatedly did, sometimes in cooperation with one another and sometimes unilaterally, in the decades after Napoleon's defeat. It was this combination of aspiration, vigilance, and balance that made the Concert work. The key, according to the scholars Alexander George and Gordon Craig, was that "the new order was in a sense given both a constitution and a constitutional watchdog—a balance of power . . . and a concert of powers to watch over it."[23]

Like all orders, this one had limitations. The profoundly conservative nature of the system could have the effect of stifling not just revolutionary change but liberal political evolution. In this vein, the more reactionary members of the Concert would subsequently cite the preservation of peace as an excuse to stamp out threats to monarchical rule. The post-1815 order was also sharply biased against the interests of small states; demands for international equality or self-determination were often sacrificed to the imperatives of great-power peace. A main principle of the system, Castlereagh wrote, was "that the inferior States must be summoned to assist, or pay the forfeit of resistance."[24] Over time, moreover, the European concert may simply have channeled geopolitical competition outward; it is probably no coincidence that a frenzy of European imperial expansion occurred as the nineteenth century went on. Nor did the system even fully prevent wars, let alone peacetime contention, among the great powers. The Quadruple Alliance itself broke down after only a few years, leading to a far longer period in which shifting coalitions maneuvered against one another, both responding to and generating continual geopolitical crises. Most notably, the Crimean War of the 1850s and the wars of German reunification between 1864 and 1871 showed that the potential for great-power violence persisted even in an era of relative peace.

Yet if the Concert did not achieve perfection, it did, as Henry Kissinger wrote, provide remarkable stability.[25] There were no wars among the European great powers for nearly forty years after Vienna, and when the Crimean War broke out in 1853, the leading powers took action to prevent its spread. Otto von Bismarck's Germany entered into three different wars over the course of just seven years starting in 1864, yet Prussia nonetheless restrained itself from seeking continental domination. European diplomacy was never free from jostling or coercion, but the Concert resolved or simply stifled myriad conflicts that might otherwise have escalated.

The crowning achievement of the Concert, then, was that there was no general European war between 1815 and 1914. For all the inevitable limitations, the historian Paul Schroeder has written, "It remains remarkable that such results could be achieved at all—that 19th century statesmen could, with a certain minimum of good will and effort, repeatedly reach viable, agreed-upon outcomes to hotly disputed critical problems."[26] Of all the factors that produced those results, foremost was the hard-won recognition that the likely alternative was a resumption of bitter upheaval.

III

There is, however, another kind of response to tragedy. If knowledge of tragedy can have an invigorating effect on those willing to fully profit from its lessons, it can also be enervating, even crippling to effective statecraft. After all, great efforts and prolonged exertions can ultimately lead to exhaustion and cause nations to flinch from the necessary application of power. Too much experience with a tragic world can tempt leaders and citizens to seek refuge in withdrawal, appeasement, or utopianism. Such impulses are only human, and quite understandable after a period of trauma. Yet when they morph into an unwillingness to defend an existing order under assault, the results can themselves be tragic.

        In this regard, the aftermath of World War I stands as the cautionary example. That conflict caused a greater spasm of violence than any previous upheaval, and inspired a near universal conviction that such carnage must never happen again. Yet the years thereafter did not see an effective order-building project in the mold of Westphalia or the Concert of Europe. Rather, they saw a well-meaning but quixotic attempt to escape the harsh constraints of power politics, followed by a catastrophic paralysis in the face of rising dangers.

The embodiment of the first tendency was Woodrow Wilson. Wilson was hardly the only person who believed that World War I must be "the war to end all wars": the rapturous public reception he received in Europe and elsewhere after the war testifies to the widespread popularity of his ideas.[27] But he was surely its most eloquent advocate. Wilson had no lack of appreciation for tragedy, and his vision for the postwar world was deeply rooted in his revulsion at the great horror that had befallen humanity in this "most terrible and disastrous of all wars."[28] His solution, breathtaking in its ambition, was to create a fundamentally new world order that would allow international society to break free of the depravities that, he believed, had ushered in such a cataclysm in the first place.

In his Fourteen Points speech in January 1918, Wilson promoted what we would now call a liberal international order—one that sought to address the perceived causes of instability and aggression by promoting national self-determination and disarmament, enshrining a liberal trading system and freedom of the seas, strengthening international law, and creating a global organization that would arbitrate grievances and thwart conquest.[29] Most important, Wilson shunned the idea that statecraft should consist of the search for equilibrium and the pursuit of national self-interest, arguing instead that the international community must stand on moral principle and practice collective security. "There must be, not a balance of power, but a community of power," he told the Senate in 1917; "not organized rivalries, but an organized common peace."[30]

This "community of power" sounded, at least superficially, somewhat similar to what had emerged after Westphalia and Vienna. It also featured an unprecedented leadership role for the United States not just as the conscience of humanity, but as a coordinator and convener of collective action. Crucially, however, the primary currency of power in Wilson's new order would shift from military force to reason and morality. "We are depending primarily and chiefly upon one great force, and that is the moral force of the public opinion of the world," Wilson informed his fellow leaders at the Versailles peace conference.[31] If coercion was required, it would be undertaken on behalf of humanity as a whole through the unanimous action of an international community. There could be no going back, no return to the old ways of secret diplomacy, shifting coalitions, and cold-eyed geopolitical competition. For Wilson, a world in which common rules could be identified and accepted, international moral opinion could restrain threats, and nations could cooperate on the basis of the global good was the prerequisite for escaping future tragedies. Once this true peace was achieved, he promised, "Men in khaki will not have to cross the seas again."[32]

At Versailles, however, Wilson's desire for a transformative peace collided both with his own animus against German militarism and with the desires of America's European allies— namely France—for a more punitive settlement. For French prime minister Georges Clemenceau, the cause of World War I was not the existence of the balance of power, but its breakdown under pressure from a rising Germany. The solution was to reduce German power and aggressively enforce that outcome over time. "If we have no means of imposing our will," he warned, "everything will slip away bit by bit."[33]

The resulting settlement was an awkward hybrid. The Treaty of Versailles saddled Germany with the blame for World War I, while also seeking to contain future German militarism through restrictive measures. The treaty adjusted territorial boundaries in Europe in an attempt to create geopolitical buffers around Germany, authorized the allied occupation of the Rhineland for up to fifteen years, and stripped Germany of its overseas possessions. It called for strict curbs on Germany's armed forces and required the German government to pay reparations to the Allies.

Yet the treaty was not as harsh as sometimes believed, because it neither permanently dismembered Germany nor permanently crushed its economic capacity. The treaty, moreover, aimed to do much more than just punish Germany, because it reflected Wilson's spirit and many of his guiding ideas. Among other things, the treaty provided for an unprecedented degree of national self-determination within Europe; it essentially codified the destruction of four European empires by blessing the emergence of smaller independent states. Most notably, the treaty created the League of Nations, a body that built on earlier precedents and ideas—including those advanced by Grotius—yet nonetheless represented a revolutionary effort to forge an international community dedicated to confronting aggressors and preserving the peace. "The treaty constitutes nothing less than a world settlement," Wilson declared upon his return to America in July 1919. It marked a visionary effort "to get away from the bad influences, the illegitimate purposes, the demoralizing ambitions, the international counsels and expedients out of which the sinister designs of Germany had sprung as a natural growth."[34] The trouble, however, was that the settlement Wilson did so much to shape contained the seeds of future upheavals, precisely because it—like the president himself—was not attentive enough to the tragic geopolitics he aimed to escape.

The settlement left Germany deeply embittered but mostly intact and therefore only temporarily constrained—a combination that practically ensured future revisionism. In fact, Germany's geopolitical position had arguably been *enhanced* by the end of the war. Before 1914, Germany had been surrounded by great powers: the Russians, the Austro-Hungarians, and the French. By 1919, the Communist revolution in Russia and the breakup of the Austro-Hungarian Empire had left an exhausted France as Germany's only formidable neighbor. The triumph of self-determination, meanwhile, was simply encouraging German revanchism: first, by surrounding Germany with weak states in the east, and second, by giving its future leaders a pretext for seeking to assert control over foreign lands—in Austria, Czechoslovakia, and Poland—where ethnic Germans were numerous.[35]

For its part, the League of Nations was an indisputably progressive effort to safeguard the peace, but it also suffered from critical flaws. In particular, it left the two most powerful European countries—Germany and the Soviet Union—on the outside of a settlement they had great incentive to disrupt. Moreover, its collective security role hinged on the assumption that its leading members could act unanimously in the face of aggression, a Wilsonian conceit that would prove impossible to realize. The Peace of Westphalia and the Concert of Europe had proven comparatively successful because they rested on both a commitment to shared values *and* a stable geopolitical foundation. The post–World War I settlement, by contrast, was biased toward revanchism and instability. "This is not a peace," Marshal Ferdinand Foch, the Supreme Allied Commander during World War I, declared. "It is an armistice for twenty years."[36] When the U.S. Senate declined to ratify American participation in the League, in part because of Wilson's obstinate refusal to accept any conditions on U.S. involvement, the postwar system became more precarious still.

That rejection was the product of another type of American escapism in the interwar era—the tendency to withdraw at a time when there appeared to be no immediate threats to U.S. security. Domestic opposition to the League and other parts of the Versailles settlement arose from a variety of concerns: that they would undermine U.S. sovereignty, usurp Congress's constitutional prerogatives with respect to declaring war, and abrogate the tradition of strategic non-entanglement in Europe. Underlying all this, however, was a sense of strategic complacency brought on by the fact that, with Germany's defeat, geopolitical dangers to America seemed to have retreated far over the horizon. Had Wilson been more of a political realist, he might nonetheless have salvaged a compromise with the treaty's more moderate opponents and thereby preserved a strong, if modified, American leadership role in the order he sought to create. In the event, however, the combination of domestic reluctance and Wilsonian intransigence ensured that the Senate eventually rejected American participation in the League. The United States would stay deeply involved economically in Europe during the 1920s, but it never committed strategically either to the community of power Wilson envisioned or to a more traditional balance of power that might have better underwritten the peace.[37]

These escapist tendencies persisted into the interwar era, with mostly pernicious results. Wilson's League may have been defeated at home, but his core ideas remained influential both in the United States and abroad. Indeed, leading thinkers often found Wilson's thesis more persuasive than Clemenceau's—they argued that the problem was not that the balance of power had collapsed but that such a mechanism had ever been relied upon. They therefore determined to set aside the traditional instruments of statecraft in hopes that moral pressure and communal adherence to liberal principles would make war a thing of the past. This movement was exemplified by the myriad disarmament conferences that followed World War I, and by the signing of the Kellogg-Briand Pact of 1928, which outlawed war as an instrument of national policy. "This should be a day of rejoicing among the nations of the world," the *Washington Star* opined after the conclusion of that agreement. War, it appeared, was being banished into illegality.[38]

George Kennan would later describe this period of American statecraft as "utopian in its expectations, legalistic in its concept of methodology, moralistic in the demands it seemed to place on others, and self-righteous in the degree of high-mindedness and rectitude it imputed to ourselves."[39] War was no longer to be prevented through deterrence, alliances, and the willingness to use force, but through the willingness to abjure precisely these measures. Other Americans, disillusioned by the failure of the postwar settlement to live up to Wilson's grand ambitions, or simply convinced that the geopolitical sky would remain cloudless for years to come, were happy to "return to normalcy" and steer clear of European security matters. All of these impulses—idealism, cynicism, and disengagement—were understandable responses to World War I. All, unfortunately, did more to weaken than fortify the constraints on future aggression.

The same could be said of another response to the tragedy of World War I—the democratic powers' unwillingness to forcefully resist growing challenges to the settlement they had created. During the 1920s, memories of the last war were strong, but the dangers of the next one still seemed largely hypothetical. Over the course of the 1930s, the international landscape darkened. The world sank into depression; protectionism ran rampant as international cooperation collapsed and nations pursued beggar-thy-neighbor policies. More ominous still, aggressive authoritarianism returned in Europe and Asia alike.

Radical ideologies flourished in some of the most powerful states on earth; the fascist nations armed themselves and used violence and coercion to alter the status quo from Manchuria to Central Europe. One by one the advances accumulated; slowly but unmistakably the geopolitical balance shifted against the democratic powers. Despite all this, the democracies often seemed frozen, unable to stir themselves to multilateral action or an effective response. The United States remained geopolitically absent as the situation in Europe progressively worsened; the other Western democracies mostly sought to avoid confrontation until 1939, *after* Hitler had built up great strength and momentum. As Joseph Goebbels, Hitler's propaganda chief, later remarked, "They let us through the danger zone. . . . They left us alone and let us slip through the risky zone and we were able to sail around all dangerous reefs. And when we were done and well armed, better than they, then they started the war."[40]

Far from moving aggressively to thwart the revisionist powers, the democracies often handcuffed themselves strategically. The French adopted a military system that made it nearly impossible to use force absent general mobilization; that requirement, in turn, made even the limited use of force almost inconceivable in the 1930s. The British slashed real defense expenditures to pay for the rising costs of social services. In absolute terms, the money spent on the army and navy hardly increased between 1913 and 1932, despite the vast diminution of purchasing power caused by two decades' worth of inflation.[41] Into the early 1930s, defense budgets reflected the assumption that no major conflict would occur for at least a decade—a rule that gave London tremendous incentive to avoid such a confrontation.

The interwar statesmen were not cowards or fools. There were many reasons, all seemingly plausible at the time, why the democracies adopted a posture that appears so disastrously naïve and misguided in retrospect. Collective action was hard to organize amid divergent national interests and the economic rivalries caused by depression and protectionism. Feelings of guilt that the postwar peace had been too harsh discouraged confrontation, while budgetary pressures and desires for normalcy inhibited rearmament. There persisted a strong Enlightenment belief in the power of dialogue and diplomacy to resolve disagreements. Even in the late 1930s, British prime minister Neville Chamberlain would say that "if we could only sit down at a table with the Germans and run through all their complaints and claims with a pencil, this would greatly relieve all tensions."[42] And, as is often the case in international politics, citizens and leaders found it difficult to understand how crises occurring in faraway places, or involving seemingly abstract principles such as nonaggression, really mattered to their own security.

Yet the most fundamental factor was simply that all of the democratic powers were deeply scarred by memories of what had come before and seized with fear that another great conflict might occur. Upon returning from Versailles in 1919, Walter Lippmann had concluded that "we seem to be the most frightened lot of victors that the world ever saw."[43] Throughout the interwar period, the haunting memory of World War I hung over the Western powers, menacing them with visions of new destruction should conflict return.

Central to these fears were the jaded interpretations of World War I that increasingly took hold in the 1920s and 1930s. In the United States, historical revisionism took the form of accusations that the "merchants of death"—the arms industry and the financial sector—had manipulated America into joining a costly war that did not serve its national interests. By 1937, a full 70 percent of Americans polled believed that entering the war had been a mistake.[44] In Europe, a generation of disillusioned observers argued that the great nations of the world had stumbled into a catastrophic conflict that none of them had wanted or fully anticipated, and from which none of them had benefited. As David Lloyd George wrote in his *Memoirs,* "The nations slithered over the brink into the boiling cauldron of war without any trace of apprehension or dismay."[45] According to this interpretation, a willingness to act boldly in the face of crisis led not to stability and deterrence but to a deadly escalatory spiral. The implication was that the greatest risk of another awful conflagration lay in overreacting rather than underreacting to threats.

Indeed, World War I had been so searing an experience— even for the victors—that it convinced many thinkers and statesmen that *nothing* could be worse than another major struggle. Stanley Baldwin, three times prime minister of England between 1923 and 1937, thought that the war had demonstrated "how thin is the crust of civilisation on which this generation is walking," and he frequently declared that another conflict would plunge the world into an unrecoverable abyss.[46] This attitude permeated Western society and politics in the years preceding World War II.

It was evident in the infamous resolution of the Oxford Union in 1934 that its members would fight for neither king nor country, and in the profusion of antiwar literature that emerged on both sides of the Atlantic in the 1920s and 1930s. "They wrote in the old days that it is sweet and fitting to die for one's country," Ernest Hemingway wrote in 1935. In modern war, however, "You will die like a dog for no good reason."[47] It was evident in the series of Neutrality Acts passed by the U.S. Congress out of conviction that the greatest danger to America was not passivity but entanglement in another European war. It was evident in France's reluctance to use or even threaten force against Hitler when his troops reoccupied the Rhineland in 1936, despite the extreme weakness of Berlin's position at that time.

Finally, it was evident in the crippling fear that the result of another war would be to lose another generation of soldiers in the fields of France and a great mass of civilians to indiscriminate terror attacks from the air. British foreign secretary Lord Halifax put the basic attitude bluntly in explaining the government's reluctance to push Germany too hard, stating that "he could not feel we were justified in embarking on an action which would result in such untold suffering."[48] Or as Neville Chamberlain stated, more infamously, at the time of the Munich crisis, "How horrible, fantastic, incredible it is that we should be digging trenches and trying on gas masks here because of a quarrel in a faraway country between people of whom we know nothing."[49] Tragedy, for the interwar generation, was not a source of resolve in the face of danger. It was an inducement to an inaction that contributed, in its turn, to still greater horrors to come.

IV

The great achievements of Westphalia and the Concert of Europe flowed from the fact that the leading powers of these eras were able to turn an acquaintance with tragedy into the mixture of diplomatic creativity and strategic determination necessary to hold dangerous forces at bay. The great failure of the interwar period was that the democracies were too often paralyzed by the past. Donald Kagan concluded his sweeping book *On the Origins of War and the Preservation of Peace* with the declaration that "a persistent and repeated error through the ages has been the failure to understand that the preservation of peace requires active effort, planning, the expenditure of resources, and sacrifices, just as war does."[50] This is a lesson that too many in the interwar era forgot in their efforts to escape, rather than confront, the tragic patterns of global politics. In doing so, however, they helped ensure that their post–World War II successors would not make the same mistake.

4
The Great Escape

With the benefit of hindsight, it is easy to see the year 1945 as a bright historical dividing line— a decisive break between the horrific global wars that plagued the first half of the twentieth century and the era of relative international peace, economic prosperity, and democratic dominance that dawned in the second. At the time, however, it hardly seemed obvious that the course of human affairs was on the verge of changing for the better. How could it have been, given the recurring breakdowns of international stability over the previous thirty years, the disorder and conflict that menaced the early postwar environment, and the pervasive fear that the defeat of one aggressive totalitarian ideology might simply have paved the way for the triumph of another? Far from being optimistic about the trajectory of global affairs, many informed observers believed that the momentum toward catastrophe was increasing.

"The end of everything we call life is close at hand and cannot be evaded," H. G. Wells predicted shortly before his death in 1946. Mankind had proven "the most foolish vermin that have ever overrun the earth." "As long as there are sovereign nations possessing great power," Albert Einstein agreed, "war is inevitable." Joseph Grew, one of America's most distinguished diplomats, warned just after World War II that a third global conflict—between Washington and Moscow—was "as certain as anything in this world."[1] And in 1950, the British historian Arnold Toynbee, surveying the depressing sweep of the early twentieth century, forecast that the worst was still to come. "In our recent Western history war has been following an ascending order of intensity; and to-day it is already apparent that the War of 1939–1945 was not the climax of this crescendo movement," he wrote. "If the series continues, the progression will indubitably be carried over to higher terms, until the process of intensifying horrors of war is one day brought to an end by the self-annihilation of war-making society."[2] Tragedy, Toynbee and so many contemporaries believed, was inescapable.

Toynbee and his fellow pessimists were poor prophets, fortunately, and we now know that the post-1945 era marked not the climax of catastrophe but the birth of something better. Even the nomenclature we use to describe this period is telling. The years after 1945 are now viewed not as another *pre*war or *inter*war era, as was often feared at the time, but as a *post*war era that has lasted over seven decades and counting.[3] This era has seen dramatic advances in the spread of democracy and respect for basic human rights; it has witnessed unprecedented gains in global wealth and well-being. Above all, it has been defined by the absence of the great-power wars that previously shook the international system, and by the geopolitical supremacy of the democracies rather than their totalitarian rivals. As Eric Hobsbawm observed, the postwar era is rightly considered a new "golden age," one whose virtues are all the more striking when compared with the prior "age of catastrophe."[4]

This achievement rested, in no small part, on the enormously ambitious—and enormously costly—order-building project that America, in concert with its friends and partners, undertook after World War II. That project is now widely, if hardly universally, considered the most successful such endeavor ever undertaken. And it was rooted not just in America's unrivaled power, but in its leading statesmen's deliberate efforts to escape the tragic patterns of global affairs.

After the searing experience of the Great Depression and World War II, American leaders concluded that failure to stand up for friendly nations facing external aggression, failure to defend democratic values under assault, failure to prevent trade wars sparked by protectionism, and failure to support international efforts to preserve peace and security had produced a global leadership vacuum and an invitation to chaos. These failures directly informed the prodigious efforts and great successes of postwar U.S. foreign policy: the creation of a relatively open, positive-sum global economic order, the erection of a security architecture that deterred aggression and protected geopolitical stability, and the protection and advancement of democratic ideals and institutions. "It is a mistake to suppose that people never learn from history," Hobsbawm noted.[5] What we now think of as the brilliantly effective postwar order was a conscious response to the repeated disasters that had preceded it—and to the menace of an expansionist, illiberal Soviet Union that reminded Americans that tragedy could all too easily recur if the United States pursued a different path.

I

In some ways, the situation that America inhabited after World War II could hardly be called tragic at all. If the war had laid much of the world low, in doing so it had vaulted America to Olympian heights. In 1945, the U.S. gross national product (GNP) was three times that of its closest competitor, and American military expenditures were nearly three times those of all the other major powers *combined*. America alone possessed nuclear weapons, a navy that dominated the maritime commons, and an air force that could devastate targets anywhere on earth. Its ideological influence, as the world's leading democracy, radiated outward.[6] The influential publisher Henry Luce had heralded the coming "American Century" in 1941, but not even he fully foresaw the opportunity the United States would have to shape the postwar world.[7] America was now poised to assume "the responsibility which God Almighty intended," president Harry Truman would declare, "for the welfare of the world in generations to come."[8]

Yet if American leaders emerged from World War II with the optimism afforded by hegemonic power, they also carried the sad insight provided by recent experience. The individuals who populated the Roosevelt and Truman administrations—the "wise men" as they were once known, "the blob" as they might be called, less generously, today—had been eyewitnesses to the Great Depression and World War II.[9] They had seen how quickly the seeming peace and prosperity of the 1920s had given way to the privation and accelerating international tensions of the 1930s, and then to the cataclysmic bloodletting of global war. They had been horrified by the speed with which predatory authoritarians had gained ascendancy over divided and demoralized democracies, and chastened by the ensuing American vulnerability and global destruction. In short, they had received an unforgettable education in the fragility of international order and the devastating ramifications of its collapse. The history of the interwar period, one U.S. diplomat later remarked, "was as well known" in the corridors of power in Washington "as the Bible's account of the fall of the Garden of Eden."[10]

Not least, these officials had come away convinced that American abstention and withdrawal had accelerated the downward spiral in the 1930s, and that the United States risked losing everything it had just won if it committed the same errors again. From this perspective, America's retreat into protectionism had worsened the Great Depression and hastened the shift to trade wars and political radicalism; its retreat into strategic nonentanglement had demoralized and weakened the democracies; its withdrawal from international institutions had left those bodies hollow, useless shells. "Today the United States is admittedly the most powerful nation in the world," secretary of war Robert Patterson wrote in late 1945. "But our present triumph may hold the seeds of our future destruction" if America repeated "the tragic mistake of the first World War when future security was sacrificed for fictitious normalcy."[11]

The prospect of future destruction did not seem farfetched in 1945, because it appeared far from certain that the age of catastrophe had ended. Much of Eurasia was shattered politically, economically, and psychologically. From China to Central Europe, power vacuums were waiting to be filled; a toxic brew of human misery and ideological radicalism convulsed some of the most geopolitically crucial real estate on the globe. The world was faced with "social *disintegration,* political *disintegration,* the loss of faith by people in leaders who have led them in the past, and a great deal of economic *disintegration,*" Dean Acheson remarked.[12] Hardly had one global conflict concluded and the world risked going to pieces again.

Lurking amid this disorder was the Soviet Union, America's erstwhile wartime ally—and also an aggressive totalitarian power that was both geopolitically and ideologically well placed to prosper from misery, chaos, and want. "Desperate men are liable to destroy the structure of their society to find in the wreckage some substitute for hope," Harry Truman remarked in 1945. "We may [thereby] lose some of the foundations of order on which the hope for worldwide peace must rest."[13] Even before the war ended, the Office of Strategic Services warned that there were few natural barriers to prevent Russia from seeking "to dominate Europe and at the same time to establish her hegemony over Asia."[14] If Moscow were able to do so, whether by military force or political subversion, then the United States and any remaining democracies would find themselves in just as desperate a position as in 1940. America would once again risk becoming, as Franklin Roosevelt had then warned, "a lone island in a world dominated by the philosophy of force"; large swaths of the world might be ruled by a tyranny no less complete and brutal than those that had just been vanquished.[15]

It required no great imagination, then, for American leaders to understand that the potential for disaster hovered ominously in the late 1940s. As a result, World War II and its aftermath produced an intellectual revolution in U.S. foreign policy, no less profound than the intellectual revolutions that had paved the way for Westphalia and the Concert of Europe. American leaders rejected the doctrines—protectionism, unilateralism, non-entanglement, and utopianism—of the 1920s and 1930s, and they gradually but decisively embraced the difficult task of fostering global security and prosperity. It was no longer sufficient to limit America's strategic horizons to the Western Hemisphere, said army chief of staff George Marshall in 1945. "We are now concerned with the peace of the entire world."[16] This ethos would inform an order-building project of epic scope—one, like its most successful predecessors, that drew its most powerful and enduring inspiration from tragedies experienced and tragedies foreseen.

II

At the core of this endeavor was a concerted effort to remake the global economy. For U.S. officials of the 1940s and after, it was virtually an article of faith that international security rested primarily on widely shared international economic security and prosperity. During the prewar era, zero-sum practices such as protectionism and mercantilism had exacerbated economic distress and helped sow the seeds of extremism and geopolitical rivalry. Creating a stable, positive-sum economic system was therefore essential to the stability of the postwar world. "The economic health of every country," FDR declared in 1944, was now "a proper matter of concern to all its neighbors, near and far."[17] One common saying of the day put it more bluntly: "If goods can't cross borders, soldiers will."[18]

Although Woodrow Wilson would have shared this assessment, what changed after World War II was that the United States provided the hegemonic leadership necessary to avoid this outcome. Washington funded the rebuilding of devastated societies through initiatives such as the Marshall Plan; it even revived former enemies, Germany and Japan, as the price of creating healthy regional economies in Western Europe and East Asia. America largely created and led the international bodies— the International Monetary Fund (IMF), the World Bank, and the General Agreement on Tariffs and Trade (GATT)—charged with promoting reconstruction and expanding trade; it slashed its own average tariff on dutiable imports from 33 percent in 1944 to 13 percent in 1950 to catalyze production and prosperity abroad. The United States also served as the global lender of last resort and the primary manager of international economic crises—roles that had gone unfilled, with devastating effect, during the 1930s. Not least, under the Bretton Woods arrangements concluded in 1944, America simultaneously stabilized and lubricated the international monetary system, by pegging the dollar to gold while also providing a steady outflow of dollars to foreign countries.[19]

Contrary to the common mythology, the resulting economic system was not classically liberal. It permitted the use of capital controls by countries that had yet to fully recover from the war, and in deference to the lessons of the Depression, it deliberately provided policymakers with the autonomy to pursue social security initiatives and Keynesian full employment programs at home. Yet the system was nonetheless comparatively fluid and open—a far cry from the autarky and economic nationalism of the 1930s—and it rested primarily on the leadership of the world's dominant economy. "We are the giant of the economic world," Truman explained in 1947. "The future pattern of economic relations depends upon us."[20]

Leaders of foreign countries were well aware of this fact, and they often complained about the "exorbitant privilege" that America extracted from its economic dominance.[21] More striking in retrospect, however, are the costs and burdens that Washington bore by dint of its leadership role.

The United States opened its markets to economic competitors before they opened their own; it thereby tolerated commercial discrimination even on the part of recently defeated enemies. Foreign aid programs taxed the nation's vast but still finite resources; Marshall Plan aid plus assistance to Japan was equivalent to perhaps 5 percent of U.S. GNP in 1948.[22] The Bretton Woods system essentially required the United States to keep its currency overvalued, disadvantaging American exports, as the cost of international monetary stability; it also required Washington to run a balance of payments deficit that undermined confidence in the dollar over time. "I see the advantages to the Western world to have a reserve currency," John Kennedy would say in the early 1960s, "but what is the national, narrow advantage?"[23] Most notably, the entire goal of U.S. policy was actually to *decrease* America's relative economic dominance by spurring the recovery of friendly nations. Washington would prove wildly successful in doing so: world manufacturing output quadrupled between the early 1950s and the early 1970s, while the U.S. share of global manufacturing and overall global output steadily declined.[24]

"There is no charity involved in this," Acheson had explained in 1947. "It is simply common sense and good business."[25] U.S. officials expected that creating a prosperous global order would make America richer in absolute, if perhaps not in relative, terms; they feared that without access to overseas resources and foreign markets, the country might fall back into a postwar recession or even worse. And at various points during the postwar period, Washington would use its dominant position to renegotiate the relative burdens and benefits of the economic system it anchored.[26] Yet as historians such as Melvyn Leffler have rightly emphasized, the U.S. commitment to that system never rested entirely on calculations of pure, near-term economic advantage, precisely because the American role so often seemed at odds with such calculations.[27] Rather, the fundamental motivation was simply that American policymakers understood far too well what disasters—geopolitical as well as economic—could occur if the United States failed to foster a thriving international economy whose benefits were broadly distributed.

"Nobody won the last economic war," Truman declared in 1947; zero-sum thinking had led to its "inevitable tragic result."[28] And in the context of an emerging cold war with Moscow, there were abundant reminders of what refusal to assume the burdens of global economic leadership could mean. "The whole world hangs in balance," Marshall explained in seeking aid for Europe; there loomed the prospect of "economic distress so intense, political confusion so widespread, and hopes of the future so shattered that the historic base of western civilization . . . will take on a new form in the image of the tyranny that we fought to destroy in Germany."[29] American officials certainly aspired to create something better in reshaping the global economy after World War II. But what really drove them was fear of a return to something worse.

III

The same was true of the accompanying U.S.-led security order. American officials had always planned to push the nation's strategic frontier outward after World War II, to maintain control of the air bases and islands from which it could project power and confront aggressors; Roosevelt and those around him understood that the United States would have a critical part in ensuring international peace. Precisely what that entailed remained somewhat inchoate when Roosevelt died, however, and as the Cold War subsequently deepened in the late 1940s and after, America took on a range of security commitments far broader than even he had imagined.

U.S. leaders broke with one hundred fifty years of diplomatic precedent by concluding peacetime military alliances with dozens of countries in East Asia, Western Europe, and elsewhere; the new world was now formally committed to

defending the old. As a result, the troops never fully came home
after World War II, as they had after World War I. Rather, the
United States substantiated its global commitments by stationing hundreds of thousands of military personnel overseas, where
they manned the front lines from the Korean Peninsula to the
Fulda Gap. Similarly, the United States provided military and
economic assistance to friendly governments: the Mutual Security Program of the 1950s fused the Marshall Plan with support for European defense. U.S. leaders also openly avowed their
intention to uphold stability and prevent aggression or other
forms of Soviet encroachment in key regions, and over the
succeeding decades they would employ initiatives from covert
action to the overt use of force for these purposes. There would
be no reliance on international moral opinion to maintain the
peace, no retreat to the Western Hemisphere as during the 1920s.
The United States was now committed to playing a security role
no less hegemonic than its economic endeavors.

Underpinning all of these activities was massive, un-
equaled hard power in the form of an unprecedented peacetime
defense establishment. After a period of rapid demobilization
and austerity in the late 1940s, the United States undertook to
build preponderant military might, so as to ensure that the
global balance of power would never tilt decisively against
America and the democratic world. The Pentagon would ultimately build tens of thousands of nuclear weapons for purposes of deterrence and war-fighting; it fielded conventional
forces capable of projecting power and fighting major conflicts
thousands of miles from the nation's shores. Overall defense
spending would reach levels previously unimaginable outside
of global war—over 13 percent of gross domestic product (GDP)
during the early 1950s and around 7.5 percent, on average,
over the course of the Cold War. "Without superior aggregate

military strength, in being and readily mobilizable," wrote Paul Nitze in NSC-68, a landmark report submitted to Truman in 1950, "a policy of 'containment' . . . is no more than a policy of bluff."[30]

Collectively, these initiatives served a variety of critical strategic purposes. They provided the climate of security in which reconstruction could occur and an open global economy could flourish. They reassured countries in Europe and the Asia-Pacific region that Japan and Germany could be revived without posing a renewed threat to their neighbors; they smothered, under a blanket of American commitment and dominance, many of the long-running geopolitical conflicts that had previously afflicted the Western world. They created severe penalties for any Soviet adventurism and fostered what Acheson called "situations of strength."[31] They served as tangible proof, for allies and adversaries alike, that the United States would not withdraw from the geopolitical competition this time around. In sum, these arrangements were meant to—and largely did— avert the type of cascading instability and unconstrained aggression that had shattered the international system before, and that could easily have done so again if the world's major strategic regions were not pacified and the Kremlin's expansionist tendencies constrained.

The logic of these arrangements was thus essentially preventive. The United States would no longer be the world's balancer of last resort, waiting until the system was crumbling to intervene. Now, it would act as balancer of first resort, taking the hard measures necessary to ensure that such a grave scenario never materialized. It would bear significant costs and risks more or less permanently, so that it would not have to bear far higher costs and risks in extremis. "The United States contributed $341,000,000,000 toward winning World War II,"

Truman explained in seeking $400 million in emergency aid for Greece and Turkey in 1947, but "the assistance that I am recommending" for these countries "amounts to little more than 1 tenth of 1 per cent of this investment."[32] Or, to the recalcitrant isolationist who argued that "we in the New World cannot and will not every 20 years redress the balance of the Old by sending our sons to war," Truman's cohort might have responded that their goal was to avert precisely that necessity.[33]

Indeed, America's postwar leaders were acutely aware of how precarious and easily disrupted international peace traditionally had been, so they resolved to lean forward in addressing even the most dangerous global challenges. Throughout the late 1940s, the Joint Chiefs of Staff had insisted that South Korea was not militarily or economically significant enough to be considered vital to U.S. security. In January 1950, Secretary of State Acheson publicly announced that the country was outside the U.S. "defense perimeter." Yet when Kim Il Sung marched North Korean forces southward five months later, Truman quickly resolved to resist. "In my generation, this was not the first occasion when the strong had attacked the weak," he later wrote. "I recalled some earlier instances: Manchuria, Ethiopia, Austria. I remembered how each time that the democracies failed to act it had encouraged the aggressors to keep going ahead. . . . I felt certain that if South Korea was allowed to fall, Communist leaders would be emboldened to override nations closer to our own shores. . . . If this was allowed to go unchallenged it would mean a third world war, just as similar incidents had brought on the second world war."[34]

International order had to be reinforced when challenged, Truman understood; fighting a limited war now could reduce the chances of a global war later. To a generation that had seen two previous crackups of world order, the lesson was clear: eternal vigilance was the price of an enduring peace.

IV

Intertwined with these economic and security arrangements was a third element of America's order-building project: support for key international institutions and norms. "We have profited by our past mistakes," FDR promised in 1942. "This time we shall know how to make full use of victory."[35] Abstention from the League of Nations had crippled international cooperation and deprived America of influence, FDR and those who succeeded him believed, all in the name of preserving a tradition of independence and unilateralism that had become inappropriate in an interconnected world. During and after World War II, U.S. officials therefore traded away some of the freedom of action America had so jealously maintained during the interwar era as the price of building a global institutional architecture with Washington at its center.[36]

The United States took a preeminent role in bodies such as the IMF, World Bank, and NATO to institutionalize cooperation with friendly powers and establish mechanisms for addressing critical global challenges. Despite some ambivalence, Washington also supported the creation of supranational institutions in Europe—the European Coal and Steel Community and later the European Community (EC) and European Union (EU)—as a way of overcoming the crippling geopolitical rivalries that had long plagued that region. The EC might well "evolve protectionist tendencies" or anti-American sentiments in the future, John Foster Dulles predicted in 1955, but the "resultant increased unity . . . and devotion to the common welfare of Western Europe" was worth the risk.[37] American officials were even willing to shed blood to uphold the credibility of international institutions. One reason for U.S. intervention in Korea was Truman's conviction that America could not allow South Korea, a creation of the United Nations, to be wiped off the map without consigning that body to the same irrelevance into which the League of Nations had fallen.[38]

Equally important was the U.S. commitment to promoting liberal principles of democratic governance and self-determination. "The United States will never survive," FDR had warned at the height of Hitler's conquests in 1941, "as a happy and fertile oasis of liberty surrounded by a cruel desert of dictatorship."[39] Conversely, a more democratic world would presumably be a more peaceful world, given the greater respect that democracies showed for the dignity of the individual and the bias they displayed for peaceful dispute resolution. It would also be a world in which a democratic America would be more secure and influential.

Postwar statecraft was therefore geared toward preserving a global environment in which political liberalism and human rights could flourish. American officials helped democratize former aggressors in hopes of making them responsible international citizens; they worked, through the Marshall Plan and other initiatives, to save endangered democracies from economic chaos and anarchy; they used NATO and other alliances to bind the world's leading democracies into a powerful geopolitical community. The North Atlantic democracies were joined by more than convergent strategic interests, Acheson declared in 1949; they were bound by their "common faith" in human dignity and political liberty.[40] America's commitment to advancing democracy and human rights was never absolute, of course, because that objective sometimes clashed with the near-term imperative of geopolitical stability, particularly in the Third World. But there was never any doubt that America was a vigorous proponent of an international order in which democratic values were prevalent, and as the postwar era progressed, U.S. officials would gradually become more assertive in promoting those values.[41]

Crucially, American officials also labored to protect independent nations—democratic and otherwise—from conquest or other infringements upon their political independence. Beginning with the Atlantic Charter in 1941, U.S. officials had insisted that freedom from coercion and aggression represented the foundation of any stable international system, and that the preservation of a world of independent states represented the best protection against the dominance of any totalitarian regime. By resisting Soviet pressure on Iran in 1946, by supporting Greece and Turkey against subversion and intimidation in 1947, by opposing communist attempts to subjugate South Korea and later South Vietnam, U.S. officials sought to vindicate the ideal of self-determination and prevent a return to the cutthroat ways of the 1930s. "The world is not static, and the status quo is not sacred," Truman explained in 1947. But to permit "changes in the status quo . . . by such methods as coercion, or by such subterfuges as political infiltration," was to cast international society back into the darkness it had just escaped.[42]

The order that America created after World War II thus featured a variety of interlocking components and ideas. It blended grand, optimistic aspirations for global security and prosperity with the more pessimistic realism induced by the interwar period and World War II. It rested on a belief in progressive ideals married to a recognition that such ideals meant little absent the supporting application of power. It looked forward, toward the better international environment Washington sought, but also leaned backward against the sort of collapses American officials desperately hoped to avoid. And critically, it blended hegemonic power and ambition with solicitude for the input and interests of others.

The United States never dissembled about its dominant role in the international system, and it could come down hard even on its closest allies when they crossed Washington, as Dwight Eisenhower famously did in thwarting the British, French, and Israeli war against Nasser's Egypt in 1956. On the whole, however, the United States pursued its leadership within an inclusive framework that promoted the security and well-being of like-minded nations; it did well, more often than not, by doing good. "What the United States most requires from candid observers abroad are not reproofs that it is abusing its giant power," wrote British officials in 1947, "but commendation for such wisdom and generosity as it has thus far displayed, along with encouragement bravely to persevere in the employment of its vast resources for its own and the general welfare."[43]

It is misleading, in fact, to think of the postwar system as a solely *American* order, because that order actively encouraged—and even depended upon—the ideas and initiative of others. The postwar economic order was not purely an American creation; it drew substantially on input from the British, notably John Maynard Keynes. Likewise, NATO was not some domineering scheme foisted upon reluctant Europeans. It was Europeans desperate for American protection who first came up with the idea, and it was the Americans who were initially somewhat reluctant to join this most entangling alliance. If the United States created something like an empire after World War II, it was an "empire by invitation" rather than an empire by imposition.[44] And throughout the Cold War, it was this multilateral and inclusive character of the American-led order that gave it such strength and longevity in comparison to the rival Soviet bloc. The United States was never alone in promoting international openness, stability, and freedom after World War II; it was the leader of a wider coalition of nations that broadly supported that vision.

Yet the critical glue that held the postwar order together was nonetheless the remarkable activism of the United States. It was not until the 1960s that John Kennedy would pledge that America would "pay any price, bear any burden, meet any hardship, support any friend, oppose any foe to assure the survival and the success of liberty," but the basic ethos was there from the beginning.[45] "It will be hard for us," Acheson declared in 1946. "We have got to understand that all our lives the danger, the uncertainty, the need for alertness, for effort, for discipline will be upon us." "There is no war to end all wars," agreed John McCloy, another mainstay of the postwar foreign policy establishment. "No war to make the world forever safe. Men who fight for freedom merely win the opportunity to continue the peacetime struggle to preserve and advance it."[46] The sort of international order they sought, American officials believed, could be sustained only through heroic and enduring travails.

V

It is easy, in hindsight, to "normalize" this immense global activism—to see it as the logical, even obvious, answer to the international situation America confronted after World War II. Yet in this case, hindsight obscures as much as it clarifies, because there was nothing inevitable or obvious about Washington's choice. Quite the opposite—pursuing an order-making project of nearly global scope forced America to do an array of things that seemed profoundly alien and *ab*normal.

It required patrolling the frontiers of obscure countries half a world away; it entailed risking nuclear war over crises

involving hot spots—Berlin, Quemoy, Matsu—with little strategic significance of their own. "We have a genius for getting in
a hole to protect ourselves," Eisenhower remarked—"we are
always having to defend Matsu or some other out of the way
place."[47] It involved spending what previously would have been
considered astronomical sums on peacetime defense, diplomacy, and intelligence, and confronting fears that developing
a large national security apparatus would turn America into an
illiberal "garrison state." It required tolerating the behavior of
morally unsavory partners, as well as persistent free-riding by
democratic allies, such as Charles de Gaulle's France, that often
seemed profoundly ungrateful for American protection. It
meant subsidizing the well-being of countries, such as Germany and Japan, that had just recently terrorized the world.
Above all, it meant breaking with cherished diplomatic tradi-
tions—"we want America for Americans and Europe for Europeans, and that is a good American doctrine," isolationist
senator Hamilton Fish declared in 1940—and conquering
America's own deep ambivalence about its vast postwar role.[48]

    That ambivalence was real enough, and desires to dispense
with these quasi-imperial responsibilities and revert to a more
"normal" foreign policy were more common than we often
remember. George Kennan is now revered as the founder of
containment; less well known are his continual doubts about
whether the United States could "handle successfully for any
length of time the problems of great peoples other than our
own."[49] The Marshall Plan was not initially envisioned as the
beginning of a multigenerational commitment to the old world;
its goal, administrator Paul Hoffman explained, was "to get
Europe on its feet and off our backs."[50] Into the 1950s, Eisenhower hoped that Western Europe could soon become "a third
great power bloc" so that America could "sit back and relax

somewhat."[51] And at regular intervals—after the Soviet A-bomb test in 1949, *Sputnik* in 1957, Vietnam and the oil shocks in the 1970s—there was pervasive skepticism about whether the United States could and should sustain its outsized endeavors.

The reason America never did revert to normalcy, of course, was that its leaders ultimately concluded that it was overwhelmingly in the country's best interests *not* to do so—that the United States gained more by living in a healthy world than it lost by having to underwrite that environment. Yet it seems doubtful that U.S. elites would have come to this conclusion without their visceral appreciation of tragedy. Whatever their doubts, American officials like Acheson, Truman, and Eisenhower in the 1940s and 1950s—and Kennedy, Nixon, Kissinger, and Reagan in the decades after—were willing to make enormous investments in international order because they understood that there were far worse things than having to make those investments. The horrors of the Great Depression and World War II provided a vivid reminder of how abruptly and totally catastrophe could strike absent the stewardship of a benign hegemonic power; the Soviet threat ensured that U.S. policymakers never forgot the lesson. The philosopher Isaiah Berlin famously contrasted the fox, which knows many small things, to the hedgehog, which knows one big thing.[52] The statesmen of the postwar generation were hedgehogs. Their single organizing principle was that the alternative to extraordinary American exertions was tragedy.

VI

No great endeavor is costless, however, and America's postwar project entailed dilemmas and tragedies of its own. Almost from the start of the postwar era, skeptics—including leading internationalists such as Walter Lippmann—had warned that the creation of an informal American empire would lead the United States into unending moral compromises, interventions on behalf of dubious clients, and other misadventures that would tax the spiritual health and economic resources of even the most powerful country in the world.[53] And almost from the start, the critics were on to something.

World politics is a rough business, and in the service of global order and anticommunism the United States undertook activities that could be nasty indeed. Covert interventions, support for ruthless right-wing dictators, attempted assassinations of unfriendly leaders, destabilization and sabotage of countries deemed hostile all became part of the American repertoire. "We are facing an implacable enemy whose avowed objective is world domination," one classified report on CIA operations explained. "There are no rules in such a game. Hitherto acceptable norms of human conduct do not apply."[54] Convinced of the need to confront aggression and disorder, U.S. political leaders sometimes exaggerated the dangers at hand to rally domestic support. "If we made our points clearer than truth," in Acheson's immortal phrasing, "we . . . could hardly do otherwise."[55] Throughout the world's developing regions, U.S.-Soviet competition exacerbated local political struggles, with appalling human costs—just as the conflict between Athens and Sparta had intensified domestic and diplomatic disputes throughout the Greek world. And although the United States generally sought to create an international order safe from coercion and intimidation, its leaders showed little compunction about deploying such techniques against actors seen to threaten that agenda.

To be sure, the United States never went as far as the Athenians at Melos. It never fell into the trap of which Kennan had warned in his famous "Long Telegram" outlining the Soviet threat—the danger "that we shall allow ourselves to become like those with whom we are coping."[56] But from Central America to the Congo, from Italy to Indonesia, there was no shortage of incidents in which the quest for order brought out the darker elements in American behavior.

The greatest tragedy of Washington's order-building project was undoubtedly the Vietnam War. The deployment of over five hundred thousand U.S. troops to a small country on the far side of the world was not, except in the scale of the intervention, an aberration from the pattern of postwar statecraft. Rather, it was a faithful reflection of the aspirations and anxieties that drove U.S. policy. American intervention flowed from a vaulting ambition and self-confidence that the United States could bring security and development to faraway areas. "The task," said Lyndon Johnson in 1965, "is nothing less than to enrich the hopes and the existence of more than a hundred million people" throughout Southeast Asia. At the same time, U.S. policy was driven by the same ideas and fears that impelled the broader postwar agenda—that global security was indivisible and the balance of power inherently fragile, that failing to halt aggression on the periphery could encourage disorder at the core, that retrenchment in the face of danger would cause an avalanche of disastrous consequences. "We must say in Southeast Asia—as we did in Europe—in the words of the Bible: 'Hitherto shalt thou come, but no further,'" LBJ declared.[57]

Of course, the results of intervention on behalf of a corrupt, unpopular regime in a deeply unstable country were disastrous in their own right. American intervention in Vietnam may have provided a breathing space for other non-communist governments in Southeast Asia to consolidate their authority and independence, but only at a cost of 58,000 U.S. troops dead (to say nothing of millions of Vietnamese casualties), a powerful domestic backlash against American engagement overseas, and a period of national demoralization and division that lasted for years.[58] "The war in Vietnam," Henry Kissinger later wrote, became "a national nightmare that stimulated an attack on our entire postwar foreign policy."[59] The United States generally avoided the sort of tragedies caused by insufficient vigilance during the postwar period. In Vietnam, it encountered the sort of tragedy that hubris and overextension can produce.

Yet if hubris was the occasional cost of vigilance, then the cost was worth paying, because the overall results of America's order-building project were stunning. The postwar world was not dominated by aggressive autocracies, however badly those regimes brutalized the populations under their control. Rather, the number of democracies in the world rose from perhaps a dozen at the darkest moments of World War II to around 120 by the end of the century, as respect for basic human rights became more widespread than ever before.[60] The global economy did not plunge back into depression; rather, it entered a historic boom. Global trade grew at 6.2 percent per year between 1950 and 2007, compared with 3.8 percent during the first era of globalization from 1850 to 1913.[61] Annual global GDP growth averaged 3.9 percent between 1950 and 2000, a dramatic improvement over the 1.6 percent between 1820 and 1950—to say nothing of the 0.3 percent between 1500 and 1820.[62]

Most important, there was no third world war, nor were there any shooting wars between the great powers.[63] Instead, the international system enjoyed the longest stretch of great-power peace since the Roman Empire—longer even than that provided by the Concert of Europe—and only a single country—South Vietnam—disappeared from the map due to conquest.[64] The Cold War came to be known as a "long peace"; that peace has now endured for nearly three decades after the Cold War ended.[65]

There were many reasons why all this happened, of course, from nuclear deterrence to the striving of peoples and societies around the world. The Norwegian Nobel Committee made its interpretation of history known in 2012, when it awarded its peace prize to the European Union. Leading scholars have argued that evolving concepts of morality and international law have driven human progress.[66]

All of these factors were important, but at the center of the complex causal mosaic lies the fact that the world's most powerful country was working determinedly to produce precisely the happy outcomes that eventually transpired. On issues from international trade to great-power peace, American power and activism created the context within which positive change could occur.[67] "We have welded alliances that include the greater part of the free world," Harry Truman reflected in 1953. "And we have gone ahead with other free countries to help build their economies and link us all together in a healthy world trade." Contrary to what many influential observers had expected, he continued, "We have averted World War III up to now, and we may have already succeeded in establishing conditions which can keep that war from happening as far ahead as man can see."[68]

To get a sense of just how critically the shape of the world hinged on American policy, simply ask the obvious counterfactual questions. What would postwar Europe have looked like without the Marshall Plan and NATO? Would Germany and Japan have become rich, peaceful democracies had America pursued a vengeful rather than a restorative peace? Would South Korea be a prosperous liberal society today had Washington not come to its rescue in 1950? What might have happened had America not so energetically balanced and contained Soviet power? How much prosperity would the world have enjoyed had its most influential country not chosen to anchor an open, positive-sum economic order? Would democracy and respect for human rights have spread so widely had the United States taken less of an interest in the issue? To ask these questions is to understand their unhappy answers. Considering what would have happened absent American engagement only underscores precisely how essential that engagement was.

VII

"If you want a picture of the future," wrote George Orwell in his dystopian novel *1984*, published at the outset of the postwar period, "imagine a boot stamping on a human face—forever."[69] This was not an uncommon expectation in the late 1940s. In reality, though, the international order America did so much to create—an order inspired by a determination to escape precisely the horrific outcomes that Orwell predicted—helped ensure that the postwar era was one of the most impressive periods of peace, prosperity, and freedom in the history of the world. By cultivating a tragic sensibility, U.S. policymakers were able to achieve results that were precisely the opposite of tragic.

The irony of such achievements, however, is that they eventually undermine the tragic sensibility that produced them. They induce complacency by causing individuals to lose their awareness of the potential disasters that lurk just over the horizon. Precisely because of its own sad experience, the postwar generation resisted this tendency: it rejected what the great political scientist Hans Morgenthau called the illusion that at some point "the final curtain would fall and the game of power politics would no longer be played."[70] Yet today, that illusion is growing more powerful. The postwar order has proven so successful that its core achievements are increasingly in jeopardy.

5

The Contemporary Amnesia

If a successful international order requires a hard-earned familiarity with tragedy, what happens when that familiarity fades? The question might have seemed odd during the early Cold War, when memory of World War II was sufficiently vivid, and the Soviet threat sufficiently menacing, that most Americans grasped the geopolitical stakes. "Everybody understands the obvious meaning of the world struggle in which we are engaged," wrote Reinhold Niebuhr in 1952. "We are defending freedom against tyranny."[1] To be sure, the consensus was never quite as strong as Niebuhr made out, and over the subsequent decades there were certainly times when retrenchment beckoned. Yet the United States never abandoned the role it had assumed after World War II; periodic desires for normalcy were repeatedly trumped by fear of what might follow. Americans understood how bad things could get, so they generally supported the measures necessary to thwart disaster before it struck.

Today, however, America's commitment to the international order it built over generations is becoming more tenuous. The primary reason is not that America's order-building project has failed, but that it has proven so effective. It has been over seventy-five years since the last breakdown of global stability. It has been thirty years since the end of the Cold War delivered America into a period of unprecedented influence, prosperity, and liberal ascendancy. These facts constitute stupendous diplomatic achievements, and they are the source of a creeping historical amnesia and strategic ambivalence that afflict America today.

After all, the intensity of historical memory is related to its proximity. And at present, most Americans have no personal recollection of the tragedies that spurred creation of the U.S.-led order. The historical success of U.S. foreign policy has allowed Americans to forget that progress has often been upended by catastrophe, that geopolitical competition can be suppressed but never left behind, and that America will enjoy only as much peace, stability, and morality in the world as it creates. The United States is losing the tragic sensibility that impelled it to do great things—and in doing so, it is undermining the exertions that have long held tragedy at bay.

I

The contemporary amnesia may be an outgrowth of the Cold War's end, but it hardly emerged fully formed in 1989. For if the fundamental grand strategic decision of the postwar generation was to construct an international system based on liberal values and American preeminence, the fundamental grand strategic decision of the early post–Cold War period was to perpetuate that project. The end of the superpower conflict represented the greatest transformation of world politics in generations. Yet what was remarkable about U.S. strategy was not how much it changed, but how little.

The United States continued to anchor a globe-spanning network of military alliances; its troops still manned distant frontiers. Washington still took the lead in confronting aggressors such as Saddam Hussein; it kept working to suppress destabilizing phenomena such as nuclear proliferation. America remained the leader of an ever more open global economy; it continued providing critical public goods such as freedom of the seas and access to vital resources. U.S. officials persisted in promoting democracy and human rights, doing so even more aggressively than before. In support of these endeavors, U.S. policymakers preserved a dominant military capable of projecting power into all corners of the globe. "The pivotal responsibility for ensuring the stability of the international balance remains ours," George H. W. Bush's first *National Security Strategy* explained, "even as its requirements change in a new era."[2]

If the policies were familiar, so was the mix of optimism and pessimism that inspired them. With the Soviet Union vanquished, liberal values spreading like wildfire, and no menacing existential dangers, American officials spied an unprecedented opportunity to craft a truly global order that would be even more peaceful, prosperous, and democratic than before. The goal, said secretary of state James Baker, was to build "a democratic peace" covering not just "half a world" but "the whole world."[3] At the same time, these officials understood that global stability would not sustain itself and that the penalties for strategic withdrawal could ultimately be severe. "It is our great challenge to learn from the bloodiest century in history," Bush believed. "If we retreat from our obligation to the world into indifference, we will, one day, pay the highest price once again."[4]

It is unsurprising Bush felt this way. The president and those around him were products of World War II and the Cold

War. They understood the inherent fragility of international order and the need for perpetual vigilance in defending it. When the Berlin Wall fell, the administration thus intuitively grasped that the only way to prevent a Pandora's box of European rivalry from reopening was to embed a reunified Germany within a stabilizing, U.S.-led security system. As Bush's national security adviser, Brent Scowcroft, wrote, the "twentieth century gives no encouragement to those who believe the Europeans can ... keep the peace without the United States."[5] When Saddam Hussein invaded Kuwait in 1990, Bush rejected any hint of accommodation and mobilized a massive political-military effort to ensure that opportunistic aggression would not stand. The question, Bush argued, was not simply who owned what piece of desert in the Persian Gulf, but whether the world would revert to a new anarchy in which larger states were free to "devour their smaller neighbors." At stake, he declared, was the "shape of the world to come."[6] During the ensuing crisis, Bush would speak optimistically of a "New World Order" rooted in international cooperation and justice. Yet he understood, as a classified Pentagon planning document subsequently stated, that "the world order is ultimately backed by the U.S."[7]

This basic idea would outlast Bush's presidency, and few observers would accuse America of being insufficiently ambitious in the two decades after the Cold War. The geographical scope of American engagement expanded, as the enlargement of NATO carried U.S. influence deep into the former Soviet bloc. Freed from the constraints imposed by a strategic competitor, the United States took on missions, such as humanitarian military interventions, that had seemed unaffordable luxuries before. More broadly, both Republican and Democratic presidents ultimately embraced the idea that, in a unipolar era, it was *only* America that could manage the crises and exploit the opportunities of a promising but messy world. Bill Clinton and his secretary of state, Madeleine Albright, captured this sentiment in calling America "the indispensable nation." So did the French, less admiringly, in calling America "the hyperpower"—a commentary on America's unmatched capabilities as well as its unrivaled activism.[8] When threats emerged, in fact, Washington became more assertive still. America responded to the terrorist attacks of 9/11 not by trimming its geopolitical sails, but by launching a global counterterrorism campaign, overthrowing hostile regimes, and seeking to implant liberal democracies in countries half a world away.

There were considerable costs and liabilities in all this, just as there had been before. America never got a geopolitical breather after the Cold War; it found itself deploying five hundred thousand troops to confront Saddam Hussein even before the Evil Empire had disintegrated. Promoting globalization meant managing the international instability and crises that occasionally resulted from greater interdependence. The expansion of U.S. influence could foster anger and even violent resentment on the part of actors from Russia to al-Qaeda; declarations of American indispensability provoked complaints about American arrogance. The United States, worried Samuel Huntington in 1999, was widely seen as "intrusive, interventionist, exploitative, unilateralist, hegemonic, hypocritical."[9] Finally, America was no more exempt from errors and missteps, from excessive ambition and the inevitable consequences, than it had been during the Cold War. From the failed intervention in Somalia in the early 1990s, to the disastrous mismanagement of the occupation of Iraq in 2003 and after, there was abundant proof that American policy remained the imperfect creation of imperfect individuals.

Yet the failings and frustrations of U.S. strategy were certainly no greater than those encountered in Vietnam, Korea, or other Cold War episodes, and America's inevitable post–Cold War travails often obscured how much U.S. statecraft accomplished. It was not inevitable that the post–Cold War environment would prove to be as relatively benign as it was. Quite the opposite: in the early 1990s, some leading international relations scholars believed that the world was entering a new era of vicious competition and instability. "We will soon miss the Cold War," John Mearsheimer warned; rampant nuclear proliferation, geopolitical revisionism, and even great-power crises and wars were likely as the end of bipolarity unleashed international demons that had been pent up for forty-five years.[10] Yet for all the ills that afflicted the post–Cold War world—humanitarian crises, regional conflicts, and catastrophic terrorism, among others—what stands out is the role of continued American engagement in keeping the more positive trends going and stifling the sources of greater geopolitical upheaval.

As William Wohlforth has noted, American primacy and activism acted as a powerful deterrent to great-power conflict by creating enormous disincentives for Russia, China, or other actors to incur the "focused enmity" of the United States.[11] The persistence and even extension of the U.S. security blanket smothered potential instability in unsettled regions such as Eastern Europe, while removing any possibility of German or Japanese revanchism—a prospect much feared in the early 1990s—by keeping those countries tightly lashed to Washington. American intervention helped extinguish bloody conflicts in the Balkans before they could spread to neighboring countries; U.S. diplomatic and military pressure kept aggressive tyrannies such as Iraq, Iran, and North Korea bottled up and helped slow the spread of nuclear weapons. U.S. support helped democratic forces triumph in countries from Haiti to Poland, as the number of democracies rose from 76 in 1990 to 120 in 2000; America crucially assisted the advance of globalization and the broad prosperity that came with it by promoting pro-market policies and providing the necessary climate of reassurance and stability.[12]

As a result, most of the world—especially the democratic world—tended to partner with rather than balance against a dominant America. Even international observers who resented American arrogance were often appalled by any suggestion that Washington might cease playing its "indispensable" role. "Those who accuse the United States of being overbearing," noted one French pundit amid the geopolitical distraction caused by Bill Clinton's Monica Lewinsky scandal in 1998, "are today praying for a quick end to the storm."[13] Likewise, even academic critics of America's post–Cold War strategy have acknowledged that the world would have been far messier and more violent absent U.S. leadership. "Why is Europe peaceful today?" Mearsheimer asked in 2009. Because the United States acted as a "night watchman" keeping the terrors away.[14]

If the postwar era was a "long peace" and an age of unmatched prosperity and liberal progress, the post–Cold War era was an extension of this period in no small measure because America again resisted the allure of normalcy. In retrospect, however, it was at precisely this moment that Americans began to lose their understanding of tragedy and that the intellectual foundations of U.S. strategy began to weaken.

II

It was perhaps inevitable that this would happen after the Cold War ended. The close of that struggle did not immediately produce a sharp inward turn, but it created the geopolitical and intellectual context in which that turn could be contemplated. The Soviet demise removed the overarching threat that had impelled America's postwar ambition, just as the World War II generation began departing the scene. Statesmen who took American leadership as a given—because they remembered what its absence had wrought—were now replaced, in David Halberstam's phrasing, by a generation that lacked "the experiences that made internationalism seem so necessary."[15] At the same time, the Cold War's end revived the dream that humanity might escape the sad realities of power politics, by dangling the possibility of a world in which peace, progress, and Enlightenment principles could permanently triumph. Even as America remained deeply engaged in shaping the post–Cold War world, then, the intellectual impetus for that project was waning.

Before the Cold War had fully ended, in fact, prominent thinkers and plenty of ordinary Americans were arguing that the fading Soviet threat offered America a long-delayed respite from global toil. In 1988, nearly half of the respondents in one national poll agreed that "we should gradually end our treaty commitments and let allies take care of themselves," while three-quarters of respondents in another poll believed that "we can't afford to defend so many nations."[16] Demands for a "peace dividend" were commonplace within the Congress, and even former Pentagon leaders called for halving the defense budget.[17] In 1990, the erstwhile conservative hawk Jeane Kirkpatrick wrote a widely read essay declaring it "time to give up the dubious benefits of superpower status" and become "a normal country in a normal time."[18] By 1992, Pat Buchanan was mounting a strong primary challenge to Bush on a platform of economic nationalism and neo-isolationism. "Blessed by Providence with pacific neighbors, north and south, and vast oceans, east and

west, to protect us," he had written, "why seek permanent entanglement in other people's quarrels?"[19] In the general election
that year, Bill Clinton campaigned—and won—on the critique
that Bush had been too preoccupied with foreign affairs. Such
counsels of retrenchment did not immediately take hold, because the inertia of American internationalism remained formidable, the opportunities afforded by globalization remained
great, and international outlaws such as Saddam Hussein and
Slobodan Milošević periodically demonstrated that dangers—
albeit lesser ones—persisted in a unipolar world. Throughout
the 1990s, however, there were unmistakable signs of strategic
ennui.

Republican legislators such as Newt Gingrich and Jesse
Helms slashed U.S. foreign aid, deeming it a useless giveaway.
Constant-dollar defense spending fell from $587 billion in 1988
to $400 billion in 1999, and the United States withdrew nearly
two-thirds of its troops from Europe.[20] Criticism of international trade agreements mounted as lawmakers became less
inclined to tolerate the accompanying economic trade-offs—the
pressure on U.S. manufacturing, the lack of fully reciprocal
access to foreign markets—absent the compelling geopolitical
logic of strengthening America's free-world partners against
the Soviet threat. Impatience with U.S. casualties and overseas
interventions mounted even as Washington used force repeatedly. "Right now the average American doesn't see our interests
threatened to the point where we should sacrifice one American
life," Clinton remarked.[21]

Perhaps most telling, public interest in foreign policy
plummeted. In the late 1990s, only 2 to 3 percent of Americans
identified foreign policy issues as the most important ones facing the country; when surveys asked individuals to name key
foreign policy problems, the leading answer was "don't know."[22]

In the absence of dire threats or dramatic reminders of how precarious international order could be, public support for— and even cognizance of—the laborious management of that order began to slip.

As had been true after World War I, this creeping world-weariness dovetailed with a remarkable optimism that the nature of international affairs was being transformed. In this respect, the very decisiveness of the Cold War's end was both a blessing and a curse for U.S. strategy. The ascent of democracy, the spread of market economics, and the fading of first-order geopolitical challenges thrust America and its allies into a more privileged position than ever before. In doing so, however, they invited a return of the utopian dreams that had tantalized earlier generations.

The opening shot in this campaign was fired by Francis Fukuyama. In his famous essay, written in 1989, Fukuyama argued that the collapse of rival ideologies was ushering in a new era in which democracy and market economics would spread unstoppably and great-power peace would become firmly entrenched.[23] Yet Fukuyama's thesis marked only the beginning of an exceedingly hopeful intellectual moment.

Leading thinkers resurrected Norman Angell for a new era, contending that globalization was creating an economic interdependence so profitable and intricate that no country would dare disrupt it. Globalization "has now replaced the old Cold War system," wrote Thomas Friedman. It "has its own rules and logic."[24] Scholars and pundits predicted that the inexorable advance of economic and political liberalism would remove any cause for serious great-power conflict. The world, wrote one analyst, would be dominated by peace, democracy, and markets, because there was "no plausible alternative to the global order of which these are the main elements."[25] Similarly,

G. John Ikenberry argued that the liberal system would become self-sustaining—that it was so universally attractive that rising powers such as China would support it even as U.S. power declined. "The road to modernity runs through—not away from—the existing international order," he wrote. There was no other path.[26]

The generally benign state of global politics in the 1990s was not, in this view, an artificial condition created by American engagement and dominance. It was a sign that an increasingly enlightened and harmonious age was dawning—that geopolitical competition itself was being overcome. There would still be challenges and insecurity, caused by humanitarian crises, terrorism, pandemics, climate change, and other transnational phenomena. Yet these difficulties would unite the major powers rather than divide them; they would represent threats to all and thus encourage cooperative global governance.[27]

These ideas may seem naïve in retrospect, but they were hardly the peculiar province of ivory-tower intellectuals. Even as the United States continued to pursue a highly active foreign policy, these same post-historical concepts began to suffuse U.S. statecraft.

George H. W. Bush had no illusions about the necessity of U.S. leadership, but he played to the idealism of the moment by declaring a "New World Order" in which nations "recognize the shared responsibility for freedom and justice."[28] Bill Clinton expanded NATO and repeatedly used coercion and force, but he believed that the global system would "continue its forward march from isolation to interdependence to cooperation because there is no other choice."[29] After 9/11, George W. Bush committed to sustaining U.S. military primacy and waging a global war on terror. But he also averred that democracy and markets were now the "single sustainable model for national

success" and that great-power military struggle could be rele-
gated to history. The international community had an unprecedented opportunity to move beyond the geopolitical rivalries
of the past, the 2002 *National Security Strategy* stated. "Today,
the world's great powers find ourselves on the same side—
united by common dangers of terrorist violence and chaos."[30]
Throughout the post–Cold War era, moreover, multiple administrations based policy toward the potential great-power
rival of the future—China—on the premise that such rivalry
need not materialize because Beijing could be socialized into a
truly global liberal order in which it would serve as a "responsible stakeholder."[31]

   Both of these concepts—the desire for retrenchment and
the surging hope for global transformation—were common in
the post–Cold War era. Both were understandable in a world
where so much positive change was occurring and the danger
of great geopolitical upheaval seemed so remote. And yet both
of these notions testified to the erosion of America's tragic
sensibility. For they reflected a belief that global politics were
no longer tragic, and that peace could be preserved not through
the enduring application of power but through the transcen-
dence of geopolitical strife. They implied that America, whether now or in the future, could downshift geopolitically without
jeopardizing its own security—that it could reap the benefits
of global peace and prosperity while bearing fewer of the traditional burdens. And although these ideas took root, not co-
incidentally, in the uniquely permissive environment of the
1990s, the strategic ambivalence they fostered would be amplified by events of the subsequent decade.

   Chief among those events were 9/11 and the U.S. response
to it. In the near term, this piercing reminder of persistent
national vulnerability turbocharged American globalism, as the

George W. Bush administration dramatically increased defense spending and projected great military power into the Muslim world. Not for the first time, however, the combination of great fear and ambition gave rise to overextension and disillusion. Efforts to overthrow dangerous regimes and midwife successful democracies in Iraq and Afghanistan turned into long, inconclusive slogs that caused thousands of American deaths and cost enormous sums. In the process, these conflicts fostered a generation of Americans who associated U.S. global involvement not with the triumphs of the Cold War but with the travails of the war on terror; they touched off new calls, far more powerful than before, for retrenchment and restraint. If Vietnam had, in Kissinger's formulation, stimulated a broader attack on U.S. foreign policy, Iraq and Afghanistan created a widespread sense, as Condoleezza Rice later wrote, that America was "out of steam."[32]

So did the global financial crisis of 2007–2008 and its aftermath. That crisis did not knock America down permanently, as some international observers apparently expected. Yet it did remind Americans that their resources were finite, and it led to spiraling national debt and deficits that inevitably squeezed spending on national security. For many working- and middle-class Americans, the crisis also highlighted that their standard of living had not been improving in recent decades, raising questions about why they should support some nebulous global order at great financial expense. Finally, the crisis provoked a wave of commentary that American primacy was fading fast, and that Washington might have to adopt a more effacing diplomacy in a multipolar world. "The international system—as constructed following the Second World War—will be almost unrecognizable by 2025," the National Intelligence Council predicted; perhaps Washington should accommodate the inevitable.[33] The result of all this was the emergence of a new moment in U.S. statecraft—one in which it has become increasingly questionable whether Americans still wish to defend the American international order.

III

Consider the state of the American military. A well-funded defense has been the cornerstone of U.S. order-building efforts since World War II; outright military primacy has underpinned that order since the Cold War. Over the past decade, however, America's dominance has been slipping, and its willingness to stem that decline has been uncertain. Russia, China, and other competitors have poured money into their own military capabilities in hopes of negating U.S. power and projecting their influence farther afield.[34] Yet for nearly a decade after 2010—which marked the peak of post-9/11 military spending—the Pentagon found itself stuck in a period of deep retrenchment and austerity.

In real terms, the U.S. military budget declined from $759 billion in 2010 to $596 billion in 2015, making the rate of this drawdown "faster than any other post-war drawdown since the Korean War."[35] Defense spending fell from 4.7 percent to 3.3 percent of GDP.[36] Meanwhile, the Pentagon frequently had to operate on short-term continuing resolutions rather than the yearlong or even multiyear budgets essential for effective long-range planning. Washington may not formally have had a British-style "ten-year rule" in the years after 2010, but in practical terms it was following much the same path. If "strategy wears a dollar sign," as Bernard Brodie observed, then America was investing less in maintaining its own international system than at any time in decades.[37]

The reasons for this trend were very complicated, and also very simple. In the years after 2010, spiraling budget deficits, war-weariness fostered by Iraq and Afghanistan, and the Obama administration's decision to transfer resources to domestic priorities created intense downward pressure on defense. The Budget Control Act (BCA), a deficit control measure passed in 2011, exacerbated that pressure by forcing the Pentagon to absorb 50 percent of across-the-board cuts despite accounting for less than 20 percent of the federal budget.[38] Partisan gridlock subsequently injected additional uncertainty into the budgeting process. All of these interwoven issues caused the erosion of U.S. military capabilities. Yet more fundamentally, defense spending fell because the American people decided to prioritize other things.

They chose to modestly reduce federal deficits, avoid tax hikes, or postpone difficult choices about popular entitlement programs instead of more fully funding defense. And even as concern over the state of American defense mounted in 2017 and early 2018, the outlook for necessary long-term increases was clouded by skyrocketing entitlement costs, mounting national debt, and the seeming political impossibility of raising taxes.[39]

In December 2017, Congress passed a tax cut projected to add roughly $1.5 trillion to federal deficits over ten years, despite warnings from former defense secretaries that doing so would accentuate the long-run fiscal pressure on the Pentagon.[40] In early 2018, the Congress did agree to a significant near-term increase in military spending. Yet with 65 percent of Americans believing that the country was already spending either enough or too much on the military, it seemed unlikely that this agreement would lead to the sustained budgetary growth that top defense officials had testified would be crucial to maintaining

America's ability to uphold its alliances and project power.[41] Even worse, because the 2018 spending hike was both unfunded by new revenues and paired with significant upticks in other government spending, it seemed certain to exacerbate the nation's rising debt burden and hasten an eventual fiscal reckoning in which U.S. defense capabilities would surely suffer.[42] Americans and their elected representatives seemed to have forgotten, in other words, that there were worse things than having to reform Social Security or pay another 5 percent of one's earnings in income taxes, and that American military dominance had traditionally been what prevented those worse things from happening.

The results of this amnesia were—and remain—concrete and severe. Alarming readiness shortfalls emerged as training funds were cut and overworked units were pushed beyond their limits. Investments in new capabilities critical to maintaining U.S. primacy were delayed or downgraded. Force structure contracted significantly, with all of the services approaching— or even falling below—post–World War II lows in end-strength at the close of the Obama years. As army chief of staff Mark Milley warned in 2016, America was now risking a "butcher's bill . . . paid in blood" should conflict break out.[43] The defense spending increases approved in early 2018 promised to help address the near-term readiness challenges but did not disguise the fact that U.S. defense strategy had become significantly less ambitious. In 2012, the Obama administration relinquished a hallmark of post–Cold War strategy—the idea that the military must be able to win two major regional conflicts nearly simultaneously—in favor of the more modest standard of winning one conflict while imposing "unacceptable costs" in another. The Trump administration's *National Defense Strategy,* released in early 2018, essentially codified this shift.[44] Since the 1990s,

U.S. planners had deemed the ability to defeat two challengers simultaneously "the sine qua non of a superpower" and "essential to the credibility of our overall national security strategy."[45] After nearly a decade of austerity, that ability had slipped beyond America's reach.

Or consider American attitudes toward trade and globalization. The creation of an open, integrated economic order ranks among the crowning achievements of postwar U.S. statecraft, and there is little question among professional economists that trade continues to be an enormous boon to American prosperity. As economists Gary Clyde Hufbauer and Zhiyao Lu concluded in 2017, for example, the expansion of global trade since 1950 resulted in constant-dollar gains of $18,131 in GDP per household for Americans, with those gains disproportionately benefiting lower-income households.[46] Yet in recent years, there has been growing public skepticism as to whether promotion of that order is still desirable. To be sure, most Americans still favor free trade and globalization in the abstract—in 2017, 72 percent saw participation in the world economy in positive terms.[47] But that support seems ambivalent and fickle, because there are also clear signs of discontent. In 2016, nearly half (49 percent) of Americans deemed U.S. involvement in the world economy "a bad thing because it lowers wages and costs jobs," with only 44 percent seeing it as "a good thing because it provides the U.S. with new markets and opportunities for growth."[48] And regardless of how Americans feel about globalization in principle, they are increasingly disillusioned with the major free-trade pacts that have long represented the leading edge of U.S. efforts to advance the liberal economic order.

During the 1990s and early 2000s, major multilateral deals such as the North American Free Trade Agreement and Dominican Republic–Central America Free Trade Agreement passed

Congress by narrow and progressively shrinking margins. Today, this period of deep division seems like a halcyon era of pro-trade consensus. In 2015–2016, the Trans-Pacific Partnership—a trade pact that comprised some 40 percent of global GDP and had been the focus of negotiations dating back to the George W. Bush years—was politically dead on arrival. That agreement was opposed by the presidential candidates of both major parties in an election in which anti–free trade rhetoric loomed larger than at any time in decades. When Donald Trump promptly withdrew the United States from the pact upon taking office, only 27 percent of Americans disapproved of the decision.[49]

There are plenty of reasons for Americans to be hesitant about free trade today, just as there were in the past. Even as globalization has fostered tremendous economic growth in recent decades, it has contributed to the decline of American manufacturing; the rise of China has been particularly disruptive in that regard. Trade continues to create winners and losers, and as international economic integration deepens, those winner-loser dynamics become more pronounced.[50] Yet trade generated similar controversies and dislocations during the Cold War, and those problems could often be overcome because Americans and their political leaders were willing—albeit reluctantly—to pay certain costs of global economic leadership as the price of averting a return to disastrous protectionism and building a vigorous free-world community in which the United States itself could be secure and prosperous. As such memories have faded and such motives have come to seem less pressing, Americans' willingness to bear these costs has fallen.[51]

Their enthusiasm for other global endeavors has also diminished. The disappointments of U.S. involvement in Iraq and Afghanistan produced a domestic backlash against not just those particular missions, but against the broader ambition of promoting democracy and human rights. In 2001, 29 percent of Americans believed that promoting democracy should be a diplomatic priority; by 2013, the number was 18 percent.[52] Likewise, there are clear signs of domestic frustration with the state of U.S. alliances; every secretary of defense dating back a decade or more has warned NATO that the American people are tiring of having to carry such a disproportionate share of the load.[53] And when Russia flagrantly violated a cardinal tenet of U.S. policy since 1989—the idea of a Europe whole, free, and at peace—by invading Ukraine in 2014, a majority of Americans opposed getting "too involved in the situation," even through actions short of war.[54]

Americans' willingness to use force in defense of key international norms—as opposed to in defense of U.S. lives and territory—has also fallen. In 2014, the American people countenanced military action against the Islamic State after that organization began murdering U.S. citizens. Yet a year earlier, when the Obama administration made a halfhearted effort to rally congressional support for airstrikes against Syria after its leader, Bashar al-Assad, gassed his own people, there was no appetite for action. Obama, writes Jacob Heilbrunn, found himself facing "the most humiliating presidential rebuff since Woodrow Wilson lost the League of Nations vote in 1919."[55] He subsequently shifted course, accepting a face-saving, Russian-brokered diplomatic proposal. Although there is room for debate on the wisdom of that choice, there is simply no question that the skepticism Obama encountered is well reflected in broader American opinion on foreign affairs.

In 2013, 52 percent of Americans—at that point, the highest number in decades—believed that the United States should "mind its own business internationally and let other countries get along the best they can on their own."[56] By 2016, the number agreeing with a similar statement had risen to 57 percent.[57] In the same vein, views that the United States should "stay out of world affairs" reached a postwar high of over 40 percent in 2014, and over the course of 2017, only a tiny sliver of Americans thought that international problems (including terrorism) were the most important challenges facing the country.[58] After 2009, moreover, consistently fewer than 20 percent of Americans preferred that their president—whether Obama or Trump—focus primarily on foreign policy, as opposed to 25–40 percent under George W. Bush.[59] All of this adds up to some of the most pronounced anti-internationalism the United States has experienced in generations. Americans increasingly want to tend their own garden, not the world's.

This is not to say that Americans are fleeing the world headlong, or that they are rejecting the postwar order in principle. When Americans are asked if they support U.S. alliances, prefer free trade to protectionism, and believe Washington should possess the world's most powerful military, they answer yes, often by considerable margins.[60] What Americans are becoming more resistant to are the sacrifices and trade-offs necessary to preserve the country's postwar achievements.

Americans want military primacy, but they don't want to reform Social Security or raise taxes to cover the tab. They like the benefits of free trade, but they increasingly revolt against the dislocations that accompany it. When asked by pollsters, they say that U.S. alliances are a good thing, but whether they want to risk thousands of American lives to defend Taiwan or Estonia is a different proposition. Americans are not becoming isolationist; they are simply becoming conflicted about paying the costs of their order-building project. As the historical distance from the events that catalyzed that project lengthens, they are asking whether doing so still makes sense.

IV

It is hard to blame them, because many of their leaders and elites have been stoking precisely that ambivalence. In recent years, prominent intellectuals have argued that the remarkable degree of peace and stability the world has enjoyed since World War II has been a product of revolutionary moral advances on the part of humanity, or of breakthroughs in international law, rather than the result of tireless geopolitical management by the United States and its allies.[61] Within academia, the study of international relations is heavily influenced by scholars who argue that Washington can have the geopolitical equivalent of a free lunch—that terminating alliances, reducing America's overseas military footprint, and dramatically retrenching can make the United States *more* prosperous, secure, and influential.[62] And while it is easy to dismiss the influence of ideas expressed by intellectuals, similar notions have pervaded the worldviews of the past two presidents.

To be sure, Barack Obama was never as hell-bent on retreat as some critics claimed. He escalated one war in Afghanistan and launched another in Libya. He further expanded NATO and modernized U.S. alliances in the Asia-Pacific. He used punishing economic sanctions as well as other pressures in addressing Iran's nuclear program, and waged an aggressive campaign against terrorist groups that directly threatened the United States. "Ask Osama bin Laden and the 22 other out of 30 top al Qaeda leaders who have been taken off the field whether I engage in appeasement," he once remarked.[63] Yet Obama also reflected America's conflicted feelings about international leadership, because he always displayed a certain personal diffidence regarding that role, and he often espoused the very ideas that were undermining America's tragic sensibility.

Hard as it is to remember now, Obama's team came into power speaking the language of great-power convergence and global transformation. "Most nations worry about the same global threats," secretary of state Hillary Clinton declared in 2009. By "inducing greater cooperation . . . and reducing competition," Washington could turn an emerging "multi-polar world" into a "multi-partner world."[64] Likewise, Obama's 2010 *National Security Strategy* made virtually no mention of great-power rivalry. Instead, it focused—as the administration's early policies toward Russia and China did—on "galvanizing the collective action that can serve common interests" on transnational problems from counterterrorism to climate change and working toward the eventual abolition of nuclear weapons.[65] When confronted, in 2012, with the idea that Russia might be more interested in undermining than sustaining the international order, Obama responded dismissively: "The 1980s are now calling to ask for their foreign policy back."[66]

In the event, of course, Obama's tenure did see sharply revisionist behavior by Moscow and Beijing. Yet even at the close of his presidency, there remained an obvious reluctance to acknowledge that traditional patterns of geopolitics had returned. The White House reportedly discouraged the Pentagon from using the phrase "great-power competition" to describe an undeniably competitive relationship with Beijing; Obama continued to claim that the danger was a weak China that could not contribute to solving shared challenges, not a strong China that might seek to dominate the Asia-Pacific.[67] Meanwhile, secretary of state John Kerry characterized Vladimir Putin's seizure of Crimea as "19th century behavior," instead of acknowledging it as typical of the intensifying great-power rivalry that increasingly threatened to define the twenty-first century.[68] To its credit, the Obama administration did take some meaningful actions to respond to these challenges—the "pivot" toward greater engagement in the Asia-Pacific, the economic and diplomatic sanctions imposed on Russia after its invasion of Ukraine, and the renewed attention to European deterrence after 2014. Yet throughout Obama's presidency, many of his policies—both within and beyond the realm of great-power relations—conveyed the same world-weariness evident in the broader body politic.

Obama's administration initiated the trend of downward Pentagon budgets via deep cuts that began in 2011 and ultimately helped rob the Asia pivot of much of its military muscle. As his former advisers have acknowledged, Obama also made simply getting out of Iraq, a country he and many Americans were quite ready to be done with, a higher priority than preserving the precarious stability that had been purchased at such a high price by the time he took office.[69] He steadfastly refused to intervene decisively in the Syrian civil war, despite worries that this conflict might become a "geopolitical Chernobyl" contaminating the region and beyond.[70] Finally, even as relations with Russia and China grew more contested, there remained a deep hesitancy to run significant risks, or hazard escalation, as the means of checking these powers. As one former adviser writes, Obama's instinct in dealing with China was always to "reduce tensions and avoid conflict," a stance that kept the peace but permitted Beijing "to reach the brink of total control" over the South China Sea.[71]

Underlying all this was an evident skepticism not about the goals of America's order-building project—which Obama clearly supported—but about the costs, risks, and frustrations traditionally associated therewith. After all, Donald Trump was not the first president to publicly lambast U.S. allies as free riders, to call for nation-building at home instead of nation-building abroad, or to harshly criticize the foreign policy establishment for its supposed failings: Obama did all of these things in his time. Obama dismissed the idea that credibility mattered—deriding this concept as "dropping bombs on someone to prove that you're willing to drop bombs on someone"—even though the credibility of American guarantees had undergirded the international system for generations.[72] He made "Don't do stupid shit" his guiding doctrine, the idea being that there was far more danger from overreach than underreach.[73] Not least, Obama repeatedly argued that the arc of the moral universe bent inevitably toward justice, implying that America didn't need to do so much bending of its own. Obama always framed these ideas as a matter of prudence after the folly of the Bush years. Yet to many observers, his rhetoric betrayed a jaded view of the exertions that had traditionally underpinned America's role in the world.

The same could be said, ironically, of his successor. The differences between Obama and Trump are legion, of course, and not just regarding their personalities. Obama often seemed to think that the world was evolving toward an era of institutionalized collaboration; Trump believes that the world is a snake pit full of self-interested, competitive actors. Obama looked forward to enhanced global multilateralism; Trump looks backward to a time of unfettered U.S. unilateralism and promises a meaner, tougher approach to the world. Yet just as Obama often manifested a strategic skepticism born of both hope and weariness, Trump has mounted a vociferous rhetorical assault on the U.S.-led international order. Indeed, the simple fact that Trump was elected president confirms, more clearly than any single opinion poll possibly could, that Americans have grown ambivalent about their global role.

Throughout the 2016 presidential campaign, Trump voiced views that previously would have been considered disqualifying. He praised dictators and threatened to abandon U.S. allies. He took trade-bashing to a new level, falsely blaming the economic ills of the working and middle classes on globalization and advocating a return to 1930s-era protectionism. He scorned the idea that Washington had the ability or the moral right to promote liberal values, and he questioned whether events in faraway places such as Eastern Europe and East Asia really mattered to American security. Most fundamentally, Trump rejected the core insight of U.S. strategy since the 1940s, arguing that the effort to shape a prosperous and stable global environment represented not enlightened self-interest but a naïve giveaway that allowed America to be exploited by friend and foe alike. During the Cold War, U.S. leaders had usually seen it as their responsibility to fight the isolationism and xenophobia that remained latent in the body politic; Trump aggressively cultivated and stoked those very impulses. In doing so, he caused virtually the entire Republican foreign policy establishment to rebuke him.[74] Yet he nonetheless trounced the Republican field in the primaries and defeated a card-carrying member of the foreign policy establishment for the presidency. Americans may not have voted for Trump *because* of his views on foreign policy, but they certainly didn't penalize him.

Those views did not change a great deal after Trump became president. Admittedly, Trump's early policies were often less radical than he might have preferred, largely because he still faced constraints from more traditionalist advisers, from internationalists in Congress, and from the accumulated momentum of seven decades of U.S. statecraft.[75] To his credit, Trump also undertook to raise defense spending after years of austerity, and his administration—in early strategy documents—forthrightly acknowledged and began gearing up for resurgent great-power rivalry.[76] Yet the president himself simultaneously acted in ways that seemed almost calculated to unravel America's global project: berating and bullying U.S. allies, abdicating U.S. leadership on issues of trade and globalization, showing a strong personal preference for dictators over democrats, and consistently weakening America's reputation as a source of stability and diplomatic competence in a turbulent world. He pursued protectionist economic policies that were as likely to punish American allies as adversaries, and that were sure to set the key defenders of the international system against one another; he walked away from diplomatic and trade agreements that his predecessors spent years painstakingly assembling. From his first day in office, moreover, he gave the unmistakable impression that America's leadership in the service of a broadly beneficial global order was over, and that the nation was now proceeding down a more narrowly nationalistic path.

"For many decades," he announced in his inaugural address, "we've enriched foreign industry at the expense of American industry; subsidized the armies of other countries, while allowing for the very sad depletion of our military; we've defended other nations' borders while refusing to defend our own; and spent trillions of dollars overseas while America's infrastructure has fallen into disrepair and decay. We've made other countries rich while the wealth, strength, and confidence of our country has disappeared over the horizon." "From this moment on," he thus declared, in a ringing and explicit echo of pre–World War II rhetoric, "it's going to be America First."[77]

There is, in Trump's worldview, no tragic sensibility whatsoever. There is no recognition that the international system, and the United States itself, has avoided disaster and made such astounding gains over the past seven decades substantially *because* of the burdens that Washington has carried, and that

America has prospered enormously by helping other nations prosper. There is no awareness that the positive-sum nature of the U.S. project has been what has made U.S. leadership tolerable to other countries around the world, and that the American taxpayer has avoided the massive costs involved in *repairing* breakdowns of the international system by paying the substantial but lesser costs associated with *preventing* those breakdowns. There is, therefore, no consciousness of the fact that attacks on free trade, admiration for autocratic leaders, denigration of democratic values, and questioning of U.S. alliances threaten to undo these very accomplishments—that if the United States reverts to a more narrowly self-interested, "normal" foreign policy, the world might also revert to a more "normal" state.

If the election and presidency of Donald Trump are any indication, America's understanding of tragedy is fading, and being replaced by a worldview that is equal parts naïve, dangerous, and ahistorical. This intellectual transition is occurring, unfortunately, just as tragedy once more begins to loom over the horizon.

6

The Darkening Horizon

In his memoir, *The Education of Henry Adams*, Adams used the metaphor of the virgin and the dynamo to represent the countervailing forces of tradition and modernity, stability and disruption. Writing at the beginning of the twentieth century, he observed the accelerating rate of change in the world and noted that "the new forces were anarchical" in their effects.[1] Instead of producing unity of thought and action, these forces had unleashed proliferating, contradictory, and destabilizing consequences. As in Adams's time, the changes at work today are often diverse in their nature and strikingly disruptive in their impacts. Yet what binds these changes together is that they are threatening the U.S.-led order and dragging the world back to a more dangerous, unsettled state.[2]

"I don't recall a time when we have been confronted with a more diverse array of threats," director of national intelligence James Clapper commented in 2016; trends in the strategic landscape constituted a veritable "litany of doom."[3] Hyperbole notwithstanding, that litany would include the reemergence of challenges to U.S. and Western dominance, the return of pronounced great-power rivalry across all three key regions of

Eurasia and beyond, the resurgence of authoritarianism and global ideological struggle, and the empowerment of agents of international strife and discord. America and the order it constructed are not facing a singular, all-consuming struggle, as during the Cold War. They are facing a disorienting array of dangers, which are occurring on multiple fronts and often compound one another's effects.

Of course, this is not the only way to understand the world. In 2016, Obama advised Americans to "brush off the cynics and fearmongers." Truth be told, he argued, "If you had to choose any time in the course of human history to be alive, you'd choose this one."[4] Obama was right in one respect: the postwar years have seen the emergence of a world that is arguably wealthier, healthier, and more peaceful than ever before. But that world is now fraying around the edges, as its geopolitical underpinnings are weakened, its guiding norms are challenged, and the cohesion and resolve of its defenders come under doubt.

It is now common to look back on the 1930s as a "gathering storm," the prelude to geopolitical disaster.[5] Aggressive authoritarian powers were on the march, regional conflicts metastasized, liberalism was under siege, and the democratic powers were too often disengaged or paralyzed. We should not take this analogy too far—it is not 1938 just yet. But one does not have to look too far into the distance to see that the horizon is once again darkening and the potential for tragedy has returned.

I

In many ways, these changes are rooted in the shifting global equilibrium. The balance of power is the most critical factor in shaping international politics, because it creates the material and psychological constraints within which various actors operate. From this perspective, the relative tranquility and liberalism of the post–Cold War era were not the result of a permanent transformation of global affairs. They were a reflection of the sheer geopolitical dominance of America and other like-minded powers.

In 1994, the United States possessed 25 percent of global GDP, more than twice as much as the next largest national economy—which happened to be a close ally, Japan. The United States accounted for 40 percent of world defense outlays, and it was the dominant military power not just globally but in every key region of the world. America's treaty allies in Europe and the Asia-Pacific accounted for another 47 percent of global GDP and 35 percent of global military spending, giving the U.S. coalition upward of 70 percent of global economic power and military spending.[6] This constituted one of the starkest imbalances of power the world had ever seen, and it created immense obstacles for those tempted to challenge the American-led order. Russia might have disliked NATO expansion or U.S. intervention in Kosovo, and China might have bridled at being ringed by U.S. alliances and force deployments in the Pacific, but U.S. dominance was so pronounced that neither country could do much about it.

Since the early 2000s, however, that dominance has diminished. This is not to say that the geopolitical foundation of the postwar order has collapsed, or that the world will be authentically bipolar, let alone multipolar, anytime soon. China is gaining on the United States in terms of GDP, but as of 2016 America's per capita GDP—a key measure of how much wealth a country can extract from its citizenry for geopolitical purposes—was still nearly four times that of China. By other measures of national economic capability, such as the concept of inclusive wealth, the U.S. lead over China remained even larger than GDP and per capita GDP comparisons might indicate. In the military realm, U.S. defense spending remained nearly three times that of China, and America retained enormous, accumulated advantages in global power-projection capabilities such as aircraft carriers, advanced tactical aircraft, military satellites, and nuclear-powered submarines. "Rather than expecting a power transition in international politics," write Stephen Brooks and William Wohlforth, "everyone should start getting used to a world in which the United States remains the sole superpower for decades to come."[7] What *has* happened, however, is that power has diffused from its profoundly abnormally concentrated state in the 1990s, so the *degree* of U.S. and Western dominance has diminished.

Russia gradually recovered from its post–Cold War poverty, a recovery driven by high energy prices that once again filled the Kremlin's coffers and contributed to a more than twofold increase in constant-dollar GDP between 1998 and 2014. China continued to experience an economic rise unlike anything in modern history, with its constant-dollar GDP rising from $1.9 trillion to $8.3 trillion over this same period, as America's principal Asian ally—Japan—remained mired in stagnation.[8] As this was happening, the 2008 financial crisis cast many European countries into stagnation or even recession, while also denting American economic supremacy. And while economically rising or resurgent powers poured money into defense, many of America's closest allies—particularly the Europeans—slashed military outlays amid economic traumas and their own historical amnesia. The British Navy once ruled the waves, but by the mid-2010s it had reduced naval spending so dramatically that it was struggling to rule even the waters around the home islands. Germany was once a major land power, but by 2015 it faced equipment shortfalls so severe that its troops exercised with broomsticks in place of machine guns.[9] The resulting power shifts did not cut entirely in one direction, for some U.S. allies and friendly neutrals also prospered. But generally speaking, they created a world that was less overwhelmingly unipolar than before.

Whereas the United States and its treaty allies accounted for roughly 70 percent of global GDP and military spending in 1994, the comparative figures for 2015 were around 60 percent.[10] Potential rivals were simultaneously gaining ground. Russia remained a second-rate economic power, but it doubled defense spending over the course of a decade and developed capabilities needed to better compete with the West—airborne assault units, special operations forces, ballistic and cruise missiles, and anti-access/area-denial capabilities, among others.[11] Chinese power grew exponentially between 1994 and 2015, rising from 3.3 to 11.8 percent of global GDP and from 2.2 to 12.2 percent of world military spending. As in Russia's case, China's military buildup featured the tools—ballistic and cruise missiles, diesel-electric and nuclear submarines, advanced air defenses, state-of-the-art tactical aircraft, even aircraft carriers—needed to offset U.S. advantages and project Chinese power abroad.[12] The essentially uncontested U.S. and Western primacy of the 1990s was becoming the more contested primacy of the early twenty-first century.

The psychological balance of power was shifting even more markedly. The travails of American arms in Iraq and Afghanistan created a widespread sense that the United States was neither as mighty nor as competent as before. "America's sun is not bright," one Chinese intellectual remarked.[13] The 2008 financial crisis also had outsized psychological effects, dimming the luster of the liberal economic model and convincing some observers that America would henceforth lack the resources or will to lead. One former American official notes that between 2008 and 2010, Chinese analysts increasingly argued "that the United States was in decline or distracted, or both."[14] The reality and—even more so—the perception of U.S. and Western dominance was slipping. And as in previous eras, a shifting global balance was now empowering actors who sought to disrupt the existing order.

II

As recently as 2010, Barack Obama could observe a strategic landscape where the "major powers are at peace."[15] Yet if great-power war has not returned, the era of deep great-power peace is over. Relations between the world's strongest states are increasingly defined by undisguised rivalry and even conflict; there is ever-sharper jostling for power and ever-greater contestation of global norms and principles. From East Asia to the Middle East to Eastern Europe, authoritarian actors are testing the vulnerable peripheries of American power and seeking to restore their own privileged spheres of regional dominance.[16] In doing so, they are putting the system under pressure on all key geographical fronts at once.

China is leading the way. Although Beijing has been a leading beneficiary of a liberal economic order that has allowed it to amass great prosperity, Chinese leaders nonetheless always regarded American primacy as something to be endured for a time rather than suffered forever. America's preeminent position in the Asia-Pacific represents an affront to the pride and sense of historical destiny of a country that still considers itself "the Middle Kingdom." And as Aaron Friedberg notes, China's authoritarian leaders have long seen a dominant, democratic

America as "the most serious external threat" to their domestic authority and geopolitical security.[17] As China's power has increased, Beijing has strived to establish mastery in the Asia-Pacific. A Chinese admiral articulated this ambition in 2007, telling an American counterpart that the two powers should split the Pacific with Hawaii as the dividing line.[18] Yang Jiechi, China's foreign minister, made the same point in 2010. In a modern-day echo of the Melian Dialogue's "the strong do what they can, the weak suffer what they must," he lectured the nations of Southeast Asia that "China is a big country and other countries are small countries, and that's just a fact."[19]

Policy has followed rhetoric. To undercut America's position, Beijing has harassed American ships and planes operating in international waters and airspace; PRC media organs warn U.S. allies that they may be caught in the crossfire of a Sino-American war unless they distance themselves from Washington. China has simultaneously attacked the credibility of U.S. alliance guarantees by using strategies—island-building in the South China Sea, for instance—that are designed to shift the regional status quo in ways even the U.S. Navy finds difficult to counter. Through a mixture of economic aid and diplomatic pressure, Beijing has also divided international bodies, such as the Association of Southeast Asian Nations (ASEAN), through which Washington has sought to rally opposition to Chinese assertiveness. All the while, China has been steadily building formidable military tools designed to keep the United States out of the region and thereby give Beijing a free hand. As America's sun sets in the Asia-Pacific, Chinese leaders calculate, the shadow China casts will only grow longer.

The counterparts to these activities are initiatives meant to bring the neighbors into line. China has claimed nearly all of the South China Sea as its own and constructed artificial islands as staging points to project military power. Military and paramilitary forces have harassed, confronted, and violated the sovereignty of countries from Vietnam to the Philippines to India; China has consistently exerted pressure on Japan in the East China Sea. Economically, Beijing uses its muscle to reward those who comply with China's policies and punish those who don't, and to advance geo-economic projects, such as the Belt and Road Initiative (BRI), Asian Infrastructure Investment Bank (AIIB), and Regional Comprehensive Economic Project (RCEP), designed to bring the region closer into its orbit. Strikingly, China has also abandoned its long-professed principle of non-interference in other countries' domestic politics, extending the reach of Chinese propaganda and using investment and even bribery to co-opt regional elites. Payoffs to Australian politicians are as critical to China's regional project as development of "carrier killer" missiles.[20]

By blending intimidation with inducement, Beijing is seeking to erect a Sino-centric regional order—a new Chinese tribute system for the twenty-first century. It is trying to reorder its external environment to its own liking, a profoundly normal rising-power behavior that only seems odd or surprising against the abnormal backdrop of the post–Cold War era. It is using the wealth and power the U.S.-led international order helped it develop to mount the most formidable challenge that order has faced in decades. And it is doing so in full cognizance that this implies progressively more acute rivalry with Washington.

Make no mistake—these efforts are having an impact. Chinese coercion short of war has dramatically shifted perceptions of power and momentum in the region, while the Chinese buildup has made the outcome of a Sino-American war more doubtful from a U.S. perspective. "America has lost" in Asia, president of the Philippines Rodrigo Duterte announced in

2016; Manila must now reposition itself accordingly.[21] Similarly, RAND Corporation analysts assessed in 2015 that "over the next five to 15 years . . . Asia will witness a progressively receding frontier of U.S. dominance." The region could soon hit a series of "tipping points" at which U.S. commitments to partners such as Taiwan, or even the Philippines and Japan, become less credible.[22] As the power balance shifts, the United States could find itself in a position where it might actually lose a war in the Western Pacific—or it could simply lose the region without a shot being fired as countries make their calculations and accommodate Beijing.

If China represents the greatest long-term challenge to the American-led system, the resurgence of great-power competition is even more acute in Europe. For many Russians, the post–Cold War era was not a time of triumph and tranquility. It was a time of weakness and humiliation, a period when Russia lost its great-power status and was impotent to resist the encroachment of U.S. and Western influence. As Russia has regained a degree of strength, then, it has sought to reassert primacy along its periphery and restore lost influence further abroad, often through measures less subtle and more overtly aggressive than China's.

Moscow has twice humiliated and dismembered former Soviet republics that committed the sin of tilting toward the West or throwing out pro-Russian leaders, first in Georgia and then in Ukraine. Following the latter conflict, Russian president Vladimir Putin invoked the concept of *Russkiy Mir,* or "Russian World," staking a proprietary claim to dominance of the states on Moscow's periphery.[23] To further this project, Russia has also worked to weaken the institutions that maintain European security. It has sought to undermine NATO and the European Union via cyberattacks, military intimidation and paramilitary subversion, financial support for anti-EU and anti-NATO politicians, and dissemination of fake news and other forms of intervention in European and U.S. political processes. In 2016, Russian intelligence operatives reportedly tried to decapitate and overthrow the government of Montenegro to prevent it from joining NATO—a cold-blooded, if unsuccessful, act of competition with the West.[24] In 2013, Russia's chief of general staff, Valery Gerasimov, described such tactics as "new generation warfare." That label describes a blending of military, paramilitary, economic, informational, and other initiatives to sow conflict and unrest within an enemy state or coalition, and it reflects the deadly serious nature of the struggle in which Russian leaders believe they are engaged.[25]

As Gerasimov's writings indicate, military muscle and other forms of coercion are not Moscow's only tools. Russia has simultaneously used energy flows to keep the states on its periphery economically dependent, and it has exported corruption and illiberalism to non-aligned states in the former Warsaw Pact area and Central Asia to prevent further encroachment of liberal values. And while Russia's activities are most concentrated in these areas, Russian forces also intervened in Syria in 2015 to prop up Bashar al-Assad and expand Kremlin influence in the broader Middle East. Since then, Moscow has worked to position itself as a security patron to countries and actors from Libya to Iran, and thereby create a geopolitical counterpoise to U.S. influence.[26]

In doing all this, Russia has upended the basically peaceful European order that emerged after the Cold War and once again made interstate aggression a tool of regional politics. Its leadership has shown a penchant for risk-taking that has repeatedly thrown foreign observers off balance; it has adopted bold and creative strategies that play on Western complacency and divisions. Russian leaders have explicitly called for the emergence of a "post-West world order," leaving little doubt as to their dissatisfaction with any liberal international system based on American primacy.[27] And as with China, these actions have been underwritten by a significant military buildup that has enhanced Russian power-projection capabilities and left NATO "outnumbered, outranged, and outgunned" on its eastern flank.[28] "If I wanted," Putin reportedly bragged in 2014, "in two days I could have Russian troops not only in Kiev, but also in Riga, Vilnius, Tallinn, Warsaw, and Bucharest."[29] That same year, secretary of state John Kerry was mocked for describing Russian behavior as something out of the nineteenth century. Yet what he captured was that Russia was simply behaving like Russia again. It was asserting its great-power prerogatives in ways that seemed anomalous only to those with very short historical memories.

Finally, geopolitical revisionism is alive and well in the Middle East. Iran, the primary state author of that revisionism, is not in the same power-political league as China or even Russia. But it is a proud civilization that never accepted a Middle Eastern order led by Washington, as well as a revolutionary state that has long sought to export its ideology and influence. Amid the vacuum of regional power that was created first by the U.S. invasion of Iraq and then by the Arab Spring, Iran has been making its bid for primacy. "Our borders have spread," announced Qassem Soleimani, the leader of Iran's Quds Force, in 2011. "We must witness victories in Egypt, Iraq, Lebanon, and Syria."[30]

Iran has sought those victories by intervening, either directly or through proxy forces, in conflicts in Syria, Yemen, and Iraq; by promoting a sectarian agenda that seeks to polarize the region and create wedges for Iranian influence; and by investing in its nuclear program and niche capabilities such as ballistic missiles and special operations forces. As of late-2018, the nuclear program had apparently been frozen for several years (although how long that would remain the case was becoming increasingly uncertain), but other initiatives have proceeded apace.[31] And if Iran has fewer material means than other revisionist powers, it compensates—like Moscow—with asymmetric strategies and a high tolerance for risk.

Iran used the Syrian civil war, for instance, as an occasion to flood that country with Shia militias, to push its military presence ever closer to Israel's northern frontier, to arm its proxy, Hezbollah, with ever more advanced missiles and other weapons, and even to launch its first-ever military attacks on Israel itself. Likewise, it used the Yemeni civil war to provide Huthi rebels with the ballistic missiles that they subsequently fired at Saudi Arabia.[32] Through these and other gambits, Iran has come into deeper conflict and even violence with traditional U.S. partners such as Israel, Saudi Arabia, and the United Arab Emirates, and it has fueled—while also benefiting from—intensifying strife across the Middle East. Most worrying, it has steadily ratcheted up the chances of an outright war that could easily take on regional dimensions.[33]

Each of these geopolitical challenges is different, and each reflects the distinctive interests, ambitions, and history of the country undertaking it. Yet there is growing cooperation between the countries that are challenging the regional pillars of the U.S.-led order. Russia and China have collaborated on issues such as energy, sales and development of military technology, opposition to additional U.S. military deployments on the Korean peninsula, and military exercises from the South China Sea to the Baltic. In Syria, Iran provided the shock troops that helped keep Russia's ally, Bashar al-Assad, in power, as Moscow provided the air power and the diplomatic cover. "Our cooperation can isolate America," supreme leader Ali Khamenei told Putin in 2017.[34] More broadly, what links these challenges together is their opposition to the constellation of power, norms, and relationships that the U.S.-led order entails, and in their propensity to use violence, coercion, and intimidation as means of making that opposition effective. Taken collectively, these challenges constitute a geopolitical sea change from the post–Cold War era.

The revival of great-power competition entails higher international tensions than the world has known for decades, and the revival of arms races, security dilemmas, and other artifacts of a more dangerous past. It entails sharper conflicts over the international rules of the road on issues ranging from freedom of navigation to the illegitimacy of altering borders by force, and intensifying competitions over states that reside at the intersection of rival powers' areas of interest. It requires confronting the prospect that rival powers could overturn the favorable regional balances that have underpinned the U.S.-led order for decades, and that they might construct rival spheres of influence from which America and the liberal ideas it has long promoted would be excluded. Finally, it necessitates recognizing that great-power rivalry could lead to great-power war, a prospect that seemed to have followed the Soviet empire onto the ash heap of history.

Both Beijing and Moscow are, after all, optimizing their forces and exercising aggressively in preparation for potential conflicts with the United States and its allies; Russian doctrine explicitly emphasizes the limited use of nuclear weapons to achieve escalation dominance in a war with Washington.[35] In Syria, U.S. and Russian forces even came into deadly contact in early 2018. American airpower decimated a contingent of government-sponsored Russian mercenaries that was attacking a base at which U.S. troops were present, an incident demonstrating the increasing boldness of Russian operations and the corresponding potential for escalation.[36] The world has not yet returned to the epic clashes for global dominance that characterized the twentieth century, but it has returned to the historical norm of great-power struggle, with all the associated dangers.

Those dangers may be even greater than most observers appreciate, because if today's great-power competitions are still most intense at the regional level, who is to say where these competitions will end? By all appearances, Russia does not simply want to be a "regional power" (as Obama cuttingly described it) that dominates South Ossetia and Crimea.[37] It aspires to the deep European and extra-regional impact that previous incarnations of the Russian state enjoyed. Why else would Putin boast about how far his troops can drive into Eastern Europe? Why else would Moscow be deploying military power into the Middle East? Why else would it be continuing to cultivate intelligence and military relationships in regions as remote as Latin America?

Likewise, China is today focused primarily on securing its own geopolitical neighborhood, but its ambitions for tomorrow are clearly much bolder. Beijing probably does not envision itself fully overthrowing the international order, simply because it has profited far too much from the U.S.-anchored global economy. Yet China has nonetheless positioned itself for a global challenge to U.S. influence. Chinese military forces are deploying ever farther from China's immediate periphery; Beijing has projected power into the Arctic and established bases and logistical points in the Indian Ocean and Horn of Africa. Popular Chinese movies depict Beijing replacing Washington as the dominant actor in sub-Saharan Africa—a fictional representation of a real-life effort long under way. The Belt and Road Initiative bespeaks an aspiration to link China to countries throughout Central Asia, the Middle East, and Europe; BRI, AIIB, and RCEP look like the beginning of an alternative institutional architecture to rival Washington's. In 2017, Xi Jinping told the Nineteenth National Congress of the Chinese Communist Party that Beijing could now "take center stage in the world" and act as an alternative to U.S. leadership.[38]

These ambitions may or may not be realistic. But they demonstrate just how significantly the world's leading authoritarian powers desire to shift the global environment over time. The revisionism we are seeing today may therefore be only the beginning. As China's power continues to grow, or if it is successful in dominating the Western Pacific, it will surely move on to grander endeavors. If Russia reconsolidates control over the former Soviet space, it may seek to bring parts of the former Warsaw Pact to heel. Historically, this has been a recurring pattern of great-power behavior—interests expand with power, the appetite grows with the eating, risk-taking increases as early gambles are seen to pay off.[39] This pattern is precisely why the revival of great-power competition is so concerning—because geopolitical revisionism by unsatisfied major powers has so often presaged intensifying international conflict, confrontation, and even war. The great-power behavior occurring today represents the warning light flashing on the dashboard. It tells us there may be still-greater traumas to come.

III

The deepening competition over power and norms relates to another resurgent form of conflict—the return of global ideological struggle. After the Cold War, many observers believed that an inexorably expanding zone of free and open societies would lead to ever-deeper international peace. America's "cherished goal," Bill Clinton announced, was a "more secure world where democracy and free markets know no borders."[40] Today, however, the world is experiencing a global crisis of democracy, and ideological cleavages are once more driving strategic rivalry.

To begin with, even as U.S. policymakers were touting the unstoppable advance of freedom, the spread of democracy had stalled and begun to recede. Between 1974 and 2000, the number of electoral democracies tripled, from 39 to 120.[41] By 2006, however, forward momentum had halted. The number of electoral democracies remained roughly stagnant in the twelve years that followed, as the number of democratic breakdowns and the frequency of democratic backsliding increased. According to Freedom House, in every year between 2006 and 2017, countries experiencing declines in freedom outnumbered those experiencing increases, and 113 countries saw a net decline in freedom during this period.[42] From the rise of elected authoritarians in Venezuela and Turkey, to the erosion of democratic norms in Poland and Hungary, to political backsliding in Myanmar and the Philippines, to the sometimes shockingly illiberal sentiments expressed by the American president, to polls showing widespread youth disillusion with liberal governance, the travails of democracy have become a global affair.[43]

Authoritarian models, conversely, are on the offensive. It was pleasing to think that the world's remaining dictatorships would quietly fade away after the Cold War. But around the world, strongmen have made a comeback, illiberal populism has surged, and one-party states have solidified their hold on power. Dictatorships proved that they could learn and adapt: as illiberal leaders saw what happened to their authoritarian brethren, they became smarter, more skillful, more tenacious.

In countries from Iran to China, autocrats mobilized the power of technology to monitor populations, enforce political loyalty, and repress dissent. Across multiple continents, authoritarians paid lip service to democratic forms while refining subtler techniques of surveillance, intimidation, and manipulation.[44] Moreover, the difficulties that democracies encountered in producing robust and equitable economic growth, and in providing a sense of cohesion and community amid rapid, disorienting change, created an opening for authoritarian leaders to pursue undemocratic models at home—and to tout those models to the world.

In 2014, Hungary's Viktor Orban declared that the future belonged not to liberal democracy but to the ascendant "illiberal state." "Societies founded upon the principle of the liberal way to organize a state will not be able to sustain their world-competitiveness," he declared.[45] Likewise, Russia and China decisively abandoned or reversed the liberalizing course many observers believed they were on in the 1990s. Their leaders now tout the virtues of authoritarian governance and state capitalism in contrast to the supposed decadence and moral decay of liberal societies. They are establishing personalist regimes that emphasize the strong governance of a single charismatic ruler in a manner more than vaguely reminiscent of Stalin and Mao. And as they do so, they sense that they have the ideological wind at their backs. "The specter that now haunts the world is something unseen since the 1930s," writes Larry Diamond: "an authoritarian zeitgeist celebrating the suppression of political and individual freedom as a better way to govern."[46]

Ideology thus intersects with geopolitics, because the world's most powerful dictatorships are taking active steps to strengthen authoritarianism and weaken democracy abroad. They have opposed the spread or survival of liberal political values in their own regions; witness China's progressive erosion of democratic norms in Macau and Hong Kong and Russia's efforts to subvert democratic governments in Georgia, Ukraine, and Montenegro. Witness the way that China has exported the tools and techniques of repression to authoritarian countries in regions from sub-Saharan Africa to Southeast Asia, the financial support it has provided to illiberal governments as far away as Latin America, and the extent to which both Moscow and Beijing have helped autocratic members of the Shanghai Cooperation Organization fortify themselves against the dangers of "color revolutions." Russia and China have also utilized propaganda to undermine the integrity and self-confidence of democratic systems, and intervened—particularly in Russia's case—to assist Western political candidates who espouse decidedly illiberal ideas. Not least, they have intervened forcefully in countries that are seen as key battlegrounds in the struggle between authoritarian rule and Western-backed regime change. In the years after 2011, Russia, China, and Iran all supported Bashar al-Assad's regime in Syria through measures ranging from intelligence support to full-on military intervention. "Authoritarianism has gone global," one recent study concludes. "The authoritarian powers have taken more coordinated and decisive action to contain democracy at the *global* level."[47]

Nowhere are these efforts more audacious than in Russian and Chinese efforts to undermine the political systems of their adversaries. The Kremlin's bid to influence the U.S. election in 2016 was a sophisticated assault featuring cyberespionage and the weaponization of inflammatory information. It was aimed, write two former CIA officials, at the "disruption of the United States political system and society."[48] Likewise, China has attacked democratic decision-making in countries from the Philippines to the United States, by spreading fake news, bribing or co-opting democratic actors, compromising the intellectual freedom of foreign academic institutions, and underwriting nominally independent (but, in reality, politically subservient) mouthpieces.[49] Much as Russian and Chinese leaders believe (not without reason) that the United States has sought to subvert authoritarian governments for geopolitical purposes, the goal of this activity is to weaken geopolitical rivals by distorting their democratic processes and exacerbating their internal divisions. This is not the same as "soft power," the influence that countries can exert abroad by virtue of their culture, values, and ideas. This is something darker and sharper, where authoritarian regimes rely on "subversion, bullying, and pressure" not just to compel behavior at home but to manipulate it abroad.[50]

For supporters of open societies, the implications are dire. Those who live under the vigilant eyes of authoritarian states have felt their freedom contract. Democratic countries that reside in the lengthening shadows of their powerful neighbors have endured increasing pressure on their political systems. Democratic states further afield have seen efforts to stifle open discourse and increase the costs of criticizing authoritarian regimes. In his classic book *The Open Society and Its Enemies*, Karl Popper argued that history was a drawn-out struggle between proponents of open societies and authoritarians preferring citizens "who obey, who believe, and who respond to [their] influence."[51] Today, there is abundant evidence that this battle has been rejoined.

This does not mean that the world has returned to the intense, Manichean clashes of the Cold War. Today's authoritarians are less universalistic in their ideologies—and, for the most part, less totalitarian in their governance—than their Soviet predecessors. Yet the world is nonetheless experiencing a resurgence of governing models that rely on coercion and political violence, and some of those regimes are again working to strengthen their rule and expand their influence by undermining liberal governance overseas. These trends, in turn, remind us that the political foundations of the American-led order are being tested more severely than at any time in decades—and that ideological struggle is once again fueling geopolitical strife.

The United States and its largely democratic allies increasingly find themselves in conflict with revisionist authoritarian powers, particularly Russia and China. This is no coincidence, nor is it likely that this basic alignment will shift anytime soon. Opposing domestic political structures fuel mutual mistrust; they also promote divergent views of what type of international order is legitimate and desirable.[52] America has long sought a world dominated by democracies as the best protection of its own influence and freedoms. Tactical accommodations aside, it has generally viewed the persistence of powerful authoritarian states as an affront to that project. Russian and Chinese leaders are desperate to make the world safe for authoritarians, and they view U.S. power and policy as a menace—perhaps an existential one—to *that* project. Moreover, as geopolitical struggle intensifies, the weaknesses of an opponent's political system make an attractive target. A great hope of the post–Cold War world was that ideological convergence would lead to greater geopolitical harmony. Yet history does not run in a single direction, and today, ideological struggle and great-power conflict go hand-in-hand.

IV

Meanwhile, the system is being buffeted by yet another dangerous phenomenon—a general intensification of global disorder. After the Cold War, U.S. policymakers feared that bipolarity's

end would unleash new or previously repressed forms of upheaval, from ethnic conflict and civil wars to terrorism. "We
have slain a large dragon," CIA director James Woolsey said,
"but we live now in a jungle filled with a bewildering variety of
poisonous snakes."[53] Yet if the post–Cold War era has in many
ways ended, the world has seen not an abatement but an exac-
erbation of global disorder. As Hedley Bull wrote in *The Anarchical Society,* international politics features the continual clash
between the forces of order and disorder.[54] Due to factors ranging from rapid technological change to the disruptions caused
by globalization, the agents of disorder have become more
empowered than at any time in decades.

     That empowerment is evident in diverse phenomena that
might otherwise seem unconnected. Take the emergence of
superspoilers—actors that cannot remake the international
order, but are violently opposed to that order and can disrupt
it in fundamental ways. North Korea, for instance, now boasts
an increasingly robust nuclear arsenal and a nascent intercon-
tinental delivery capability, controlled by a leadership whose
behavior has been both alarmingly bellicose and diplomati-
cally savvy. Pyongyang has been developing continually greater ability to underwrite its perpetually provocative behavior,
and to threaten its opponents in the region and beyond with
greater damage than ever before. North Korea may occasionally talk a good game about reducing tensions and perhaps even
giving up its advanced weapons, but the overall pattern of recent
decades has been a progressive worsening of the menace it
poses to American allies, East Asian stability, and the United
States itself.

     The Islamic State, too, clearly merits the superspoiler la-
bel—or it did, at least, at the time of its greatest achievements.
By early 2018, the "caliphate" in Syria and Iraq had been battered

and largely destroyed. Yet over a spectacular half-decade run, the Islamic State nonetheless displayed an ability, unprecedented among non-state actors, to foster chaos in a crucial region, master the use of technology for propaganda and recruiting purposes, and command or inspire violence around the globe. At its height, the Islamic State's military capabilities were more advanced than those of any previous terrorist group (with the possible exception of Hezbollah), its ideology was more virulent, its narrative was more intoxicating, and its territorial conquests were more impressive.[55] If U.S. policymakers assumed during the 1990s that "backlash states" and other malign players would ultimately yield to the march of historical progress, today the backlash often seems to be intensifying.

The life of the Islamic State also illustrates another aspect of intensifying disorder, which is that contemporary instability has been occurring on a scale not seen for many years. During the 1990s, U.S. officials worried about disorder in regions such as the Balkans. More recently, America and its allies have glimpsed upheaval far more terrifying, far-reaching, and profound.

To say that the Middle East has been in crisis in recent years is a laughable understatement. The region has suffered a generalized breakdown of order comparable to the Thirty Years' War.[56] Since 2010, there have been significant military conflicts in the Arabian Peninsula, Iraq, the Levant, and Libya; there has been violent instability from one end of the region to the other. The traditional authoritarian Arab state model has been undermined in some countries and simply collapsed in others; international borders have, in multiple cases, been rendered irrelevant. Iran and its Sunni rivals have conducted a regional cold war that has often seemed more like a hot war. International norms have gone by the wayside, as a genocidal Syrian regime uses starvation sieges and chemical weapons against its own population—and has largely escaped serious punishment for it. Instability and conflict, in turn, have served as a magnet for non-state actors such as the Islamic State and al-Qaeda; they have also invited great-power competition more pronounced than anything the region has seen for perhaps thirty years. Additionally, Middle Eastern turmoil has spread to Europe, with refugee flows and terrorist attacks upsetting the stability of that continent and demonstrating the perils of contagion in an interconnected world.

The final manifestation of intensified global disorder is the proliferation of issues that are increasingly difficult to address through existing international fora. Over the past decade, global governance has worked fairly well on some issues—responding to the financial crisis of 2008, or suppressing piracy off the Horn of Africa. But on other emerging issues—threats posed by cyberespionage and cyberwarfare, the question of how to balance the protection of human rights with the imperatives of national sovereignty—the complexity of transnational problems seems to be outpacing the capacity of extant institutions to cope. It has become common to speak of a "global governance gap"—the distance "between what is desirable when it comes to meeting the challenges of globalization and what has proven possible."[57]

What ties these issues together is that they all contribute to an international environment in which instability has proliferated and escalated. And if it was hard enough for the international community to address such challenges at a time of historically low great-power tensions in the 1990s and early 2000s, it is harder still at a time of surging geopolitical and ideological tension.

Compare the painfully slow and controversial but ultimately effective international response to ethnic cleansing in Bosnia during the 1990s with the utterly ineffective efforts to address a far greater humanitarian and geopolitical catastrophe in Syria from 2011. In the former case, U.S. dominance and a strong relationship between Bill Clinton and Boris Yeltsin made possible an eventual international consensus on the need for intervention.[58] In the latter case, resurgent U.S.-Russian rivalry consistently frustrated international efforts to force Assad from power or otherwise bring the Syrian civil war to an end. Vladimir Putin even took the occasion of his address to the United Nations General Assembly in September 2015 to lambast previous U.S. attempts to promote political liberalization in the Middle East: "Instead of the triumph of democracy and progress, we got violence, poverty, and social disaster."[59]

Similarly, great-power conflict has complicated efforts to develop international norms in cyberspace. As demonstrated by aggressive Russian and Chinese hacking of U.S. infrastructure and systems, cyberspace has become an arena for cutthroat geopolitical competition.[60] Here as elsewhere, the strain on the international system is heightened by the fact that the various sources of international upheaval often exacerbate one another. And as the attacks on that system intensify, the defenses seem to be weakening.

V

In the 1930s, the upholders of international order went missing just as that order came under challenge. Threats mounted and norms eroded, but the democracies—scarred by the past and fearful of the future—failed to respond decisively. Today, the pressure on the international order is increasing. And again, the key defenders seem demoralized, divided, or unreliable.

The European allies have long represented America's most crucial global partners, but Europe is suffering from a profound and pervasive malaise. The fate of the EU is uncertain, amid Britain's exit and the anti-integration sentiment that is roiling countries from the Black Sea to the Atlantic. Illiberal and xenophobic movements have surged, owing partially to a backlash against immigration and refugees, and democratic practices are, too frequently, being eroded. Beneath a superficial unity, north-south and east-west divisions have deepened, and growing splits have emerged between those who want to take a stronger line against Russia and China and those eager to pursue closer relations with Moscow and Beijing. Britain's David Cameron proclaimed a "golden age" of Sino-UK relations in 2015, just as Beijing was sprinting toward dominance in the South China Sea; populations in a number of NATO countries are unenthusiastic about maintaining sanctions against Russia, let alone defending the alliance's easternmost members if they are attacked.[61] Russian meddling accentuates all of these problems via cyberattacks, information warfare, and economic support meant to privilege illiberal and anti-EU politicians and fragment continental unity. Europe still represents a concentration of great power—economic and, potentially, military—in world affairs. Yet as the international environment turns ominous, Europe's ability to act with unity and purpose has seemed ever more questionable.

In the Asia-Pacific, the picture is somewhat brighter, as the region's economic dynamism has offset some of the challenges Europe has faced. The region has several democratic powers that possess strong militaries and stepped into the breach when Washington withdrew from the Trans-Pacific Partnership. Japan and other countries are alarmed by Chinese assertiveness and have been searching for effective countermeasures. But here too, the picture is less of unified resolve than of hedging, uncertainty, and division. Among U.S. allies and partners, defense budgets have risen, but they have not kept pace with rapid Chinese advances. The collective diplomatic response to Beijing's pressures in the South China Sea has too often been lackluster, with China able to prevent unified action by picking off one or two of the region's poorer or more authoritarian members. Under Duterte's leadership, even the Philippines—a key U.S. ally—seems to be drawing closer to China. At the same time, multilateral cooperation against growing security threats is gradually increasing, but old rivalries—between Japan and South Korea, for instance—often stand in the way. The open regional order has many advocates, but their ability and willingness to uphold that order remains unclear.

And what of America? Here the crisis of global stability meets the crisis of U.S. policy. In recent years, there has been a growing global perception that America's commitment and resolve are simply not what they once were. Obama's diffidence, caution, and retrenchment may or may not have been warranted after the overextension of the Bush years, but they certainly fed a sense among many U.S. allies and partners that America was in retreat. "I think I believe in American power more than Obama does," remarked Jordan's King Abdullah II.[62] Under an erratic and clearly skeptical Donald Trump, concerns about U.S. credibility have exponentially intensified.

By questioning security commitments and bullying allies, by withdrawing from or threatening to tear up trade deals and other multilateral agreements, by praising authoritarians while slamming devoted democrats, Trump has stirred confusion and doubt among countries that have long depended on American leadership and protection. Large majorities of international observers find Trump untrustworthy and even dangerous, while foreign leaders wonder how reliable Trump's America really is.[63] After Trump refused to explicitly endorse NATO's Article 5 guarantee in May 2017, Germany's Angela Merkel announced that the days when Europe could fully count on America were over. After he withdrew from the Iran nuclear deal in May 2018, those concerns were amplified. A representative of one U.S. ally in Asia put it most directly: "Washington, D.C. is now the epicenter of instability in the world."[64]

Concerns about American reliability are not new, of course, and too much U.S. activism can be as discomfiting as too little. But the fact remains that there is now surging global uncertainty about the future of U.S. foreign policy, and that uncertainty is itself a destabilizing factor in international affairs.

It may promote hedging by U.S. allies and partners who no longer believe that America's security commitments are so ironclad and its red lines so red. It may provoke stronger revisionist challenges from aggressors who assess that their moment has arrived because the forces arrayed against them are no longer so purposeful or unified. Most broadly, if Washington continues to behave so erratically on the international stage, the perception of U.S. steadiness of purpose that has traditionally backstopped the international order could be eroded.

All these processes will take time to unfold, but they are occurring already. Countries such as the Philippines seem to be adjusting their geopolitical postures due to doubts about U.S. effectiveness and resolve; debates about the future of alliance with America are intensifying in other countries.[65] European countries are discussing measures they might take to protect themselves in a post-American age. As the United States turns toward protectionism, countries are cutting trade deals that exclude Washington or increasingly looking to Beijing as an economic partner.[66] And Chinese leaders appear to be sensing that their window of opportunity is opening. "China has never seen such a moment," writes Evan Osnos, "when its pursuit of a larger role in the world coincides with America's pursuit of a smaller one."[67] A period of growing international turmoil and danger is a bad time to sow doubt about America's global role, but this is precisely what is happening. The effects are unlikely to be either trivial or benign.

VI

The enduring relevance of Thucydides, the historian and former State Department official Louis Halle once wrote, lay in his ability to capture the decay of an ancient order in ways that alerted modern observers to the precariousness of their own moment. "As he records the disintegration of his world," Halle wrote, "we see more vividly what is happening to our own."[68]

Today, world order is not simply disintegrating as it did in Thucydides' day or in the late 1930s. On this point, President Obama was certainly right. The post–World War II system has survived crises and challenges before, and its fall is not by any means foreordained. Yet sobriety should not inspire complacency, because the warning signs are there and the evidence of erosion is unmistakable. As Halle understood, moreover, history teaches that the breakdown often arrives more suddenly than contemporary observers anticipate. The fate of the global order will hinge on whether the defenders of that order, particularly America, can muster the necessary determination to avert another slide into crisis and, perhaps, collapse. Their ability to do so will turn on whether they can rediscover the tragic sensibility to which Halle alluded *before* tragedy strikes once again.

7

Rediscovering Tragedy

"What chained Greece so tightly together? What drew the people so unresistingly to their theater?" asked the German playwright and philosopher Friedrich Schiller in the early nineteenth century. "Nothing else but the national content of the plays, the Greek spirit, and the great overwhelming interest of the state and of a better humanity."[1] The value of these plays, tragedies chief among them, was to be found not solely in the entertainment they offered but in the message of sacrifice, resolve, and inspiration they imparted. As the Greeks knew, a tragic sensibility is not the same thing as an acceptance of tragedy. By dealing squarely with the omnipresent possibility of great suffering, a tragic sensibility can better prepare one to brave an uncertain world. This duality of human existence—its potential for both towering achievement and terrifying descent into the abyss—was never absent in Athens. The best way to prevent a community's accomplishments from crumbling, the Greeks believed, was to be confronted continually with reminders of just how tenuous those accomplishments were.

This is something that the originators of successful international orders grasped. From the Peace of Westphalia to the post–World War II system, moments of great geopolitical creativity and vision have often drawn on a willingness to keep company with one's worst fears—and a refusal to be paralyzed by them. Yet as the Greeks also understood, the more distant a community grows from the experience or recollection of tragedy, the less likely it will be to recognize and stifle the sources of tragedy before they emerge fully formed. Today, as a result of the historical amnesia brought on by the great success of the postwar order, Americans are losing the tragic sensibility that would allow them to better understand and confront the dangers that threaten to upend that success. The United States and its allies are by no means incapable of addressing those dangers; the balance of power has shifted, but not nearly so much as to make the situation irretrievable. What often seems to be missing, however, is the sober but determined mindset that would impel the defenders of the international order to face up squarely to the task.

What follows is an attempt to sketch the key elements of that mindset—of the tragic sensibility Americans must recover. To be clear, the aim is not to outline the precise operational steps policymakers should take. Analysts can productively debate precisely how big the U.S. defense budget should be, or what measures might be taken to defend the international economic system from resurgent protectionism. There is room for constructive disagreement on precisely how the United States should oppose Chinese or Russian revisionism. But constructive thought precedes constructive action, and summoning the fortitude to defend the international system requires first rediscovering the tragic mindset that Americans have largely forgotten. Tragedy may be commonplace, but it is not inevitable—so long as we regain an appreciation of tragedy before it is too late.

I

A tragic sensibility begins with the recognition that tragedy is normal—that international orders are often more fragile than even the sharpest contemporaries realize, and that their downfall tends to be more catastrophic than those observers anticipate. In 1792, William Pitt looked forward to fifteen years of peace just as the post-Westphalia order was about to give way to a generation of total war. In 1910, Norman Angell wrote about the futility of conflict on the eve of the vicious, terrifying struggle that brought a century of relative stability to an end. During the 1920s and even the 1930s, few observers imagined that an interwar system founded on such high hopes and lofty principles would buckle as dramatically and disastrously as it did. In each of these cases, learned individuals believed that the foundations of peace and cooperation were becoming more solid. In each of these cases, they mostly failed to perceive how rapidly the geopolitical ground was crumbling beneath their feet. If, as one scholar writes, "a 'tragic' experience involves a fall from an illusory world of security and happiness into the depth of inescapable anguish," then the arc of world affairs is quintessentially tragic.[2]

Moreover, if discussions of "international order" can quickly take on an abstract quality, the consequences of collapse—the lives lost or ruptured, the prosperity destroyed, the moral depravities committed—can be frighteningly concrete. Thucydides had it right when he described what happens in such a vacuum of security and morality: "Death thus raged in every shape . . . there was no length to which violence did not go."[3]

This is all indisputably depressing, but it should not be the least bit surprising. If it were possible to construct an international system that was truly universal in its appeal; if it were possible to freeze global power relationships at that moment of creation; if it were possible for states to put aside the very human ambitions, emotions, and fears that drive their behavior: then, perhaps, the world could permanently escape the competitive impulses that make international orders impermanent and their demise so traumatic. But none of this has ever been possible. International orders, even the most inclusive ones, create winners and losers because they benefit states unequally. The power balances that underpin a given system shift over time, encouraging new tests of strength. And although the human desire for peace and prosperity is strong, countries also remain motivated by ideological passion, greed, and insecurity. The most successful orders can mitigate the effects of these dynamics; they can suppress the sources of conflict and upheaval. But they cannot eliminate them entirely.

This point is essential in considering the trajectory of the post-1945 order. It is tempting for individuals in nearly every geopolitical era to believe that their world is somehow different—that it is immune to the dangers of conflict and collapse. It is alluring to think that progress can be self-sustaining, and that liberal principles can triumph even if liberal actors are no longer preeminent. To do so, however, is to fall prey to the same ahistorical mindset that so predictably precedes the fall. Yes, the American order is exceptional in the level of stability, prosperity, and liberal dominance it has provided, and in the level of consent it has generated from countries around the world. Yet it is not so exceptional as to be exempt from the dangers of decline and decay. As the Greeks surely would have realized, in fact, it is precisely when one succumbs to the illusion that tragedy is impossible that tragedy becomes all the more likely.

II

This leads to a second component of a tragic sensibility—an appreciation that tragedy is once again stalking global affairs. The U.S.-led system is undoubtedly strong and resilient in many respects, as shown by the simple fact that it has survived as long as it has. Yet what endured in the past is not destined to endure in the future, and today the structure is groaning as the stresses mount.

Long-standing principles such as nonaggression and freedom of navigation are being undermined from Eastern Europe to the South China Sea. International predators like North Korea and radical jihadist groups are using creative, asymmetric strategies to cause geopolitical disruption out of all proportion to their material power. The democratic wave has receded amid the growing prevalence and power of authoritarianism. Revisionist autocracies are reshaping regional environments in Europe, the Middle East, and East Asia, and waging sophisticated assaults against the political systems and geopolitical positions of their competitors. These countries are building privileged spheres of influence in critical areas of the globe; they are casting ever longer shadows, both strategic and ideological, across the international landscape. Meanwhile, the countries with the most to lose should the current system crack are too often divided and demoralized; their strategic torpor and distraction are creating vacuums that the revisionists are all too happy to fill. The protectors of the post-1945 order seem stuck in neutral, or even reverse, as the attackers push forward. This has historically been a dangerous combination.

Faced with this daunting panorama, some analysts will take refuge in the hope that these challenges will simply exhaust themselves, or that revisionist powers will be satiated once their regional ambitions are fulfilled. Yet most systems tend toward more, rather than less, entropy over time, meaning that more, rather than less, energy is required to stabilize them. And revisionist powers rarely reach some natural point at which their aspirations subside; those aspirations often grow with each success.[4] Today, the dissatisfied dictatorships, especially Russia and China, see themselves as being locked in a form of geopolitical conflict with the United States; they are already using force and other types of coercion to chip away at the American order. Should they succeed in claiming regional primacy and reestablishing a spheres-of-influence world, the result would be not to dampen but to inflame international conflict. Competition among the great powers would intensify as hostile spheres rub up against one another; the security of the global commons—the foundation of international prosperity—would be threatened by escalating geopolitical rivalry. The prospects for self-determination and liberalism would fade as small states fall under the sway of stronger, authoritarian neighbors. And crucially, as Daniel Twining notes, regional dominance could serve as a "springboard for global contestation"—for the renewed clashes for systemic dominance that Americans thought they had left behind with the end of the Cold War.[5]

It is impossible to predict precisely when the pressures on the existing order might become unbearable, or to know how close we are to that critical inflection point at which the dangers metastasize and the pace of decay dramatically accelerates. One can only speculate what the terminal crisis of the system will look like if and when it occurs. What is clear is that the telltale signs of erosion are already ubiquitous and the trend-lines are running in the wrong direction. The first step toward recovery is admitting you have a problem. Having a tragic sensibility requires seeing the world for what it is and where it is going, especially when the outlook is ominous.

III

If the international order is under strain, however, it does not follow that its collapse is unavoidable. Here a third aspect of a tragic sensibility is vital: the ability to reject complacency without falling into fatalism.

Nietzsche defined tragic pleasure as the "reaffirmation of the will to live in the face of death."[6] It was just such a rejection of fatalism—of the belief that the next great global crackup was inevitable—that motivated U.S. policymakers to create the post-1945 order and sustain it through the crises that followed. Today, it is true enough that the grandest aspirations of the post–Cold War era are unlikely to be fulfilled anytime soon. Given the instability and revisionism roiling the international environment, it is simply beyond America's power—if it was ever possible in the first place—to create a truly global order in which liberal values are universal, geopolitical competition has ceased, and authoritarian rivals have been fully pacified and converted into "responsible stakeholders." Yet the existing international order, incomplete and threatened as it is, still constitutes a remarkable historical achievement. The creation of a global balance of power that favors the democracies, the prevention of unchecked aggression and intimidation by predatory powers, and the promotion of a prosperous and an integrated world in which liberal values have achieved great prevalence are all triumphs worth preserving. A more reasonable goal, then, would be to defend this existing order against the depredations of those attacking it, and America undoubtedly has the power for this essential undertaking.

It is easy to lose sight of this fact amid all the upheaval both in America and overseas. Yet the basic picture remains unambiguous. The United States is no fallen hegemon. America still accounted for 22 percent of global GDP in 2016—not far off the historical average since the 1970s—and it spent as much on defense as the next eight nations combined. When U.S. treaty allies are factored in, America's geopolitical coalition possessed nearly 60 percent of global GDP and military spending, an amount that still vastly exceeds the economic and military power of all U.S. rivals put together, and that seems unimpressive only in comparison to the utterly peerless primacy of the 1990s.[7] Washington remains at the center of a global network made up of over thirty treaty allies, another thirty or so quasi-allies, and still more security and diplomatic partners, giving it geopolitical leverage and relationships that no competitor can approach.[8] And even in the age of Trump, no rival boasts anything close to America's experience and expertise in coordinating complex military and diplomatic endeavors.

This is not to say that all is well. America's competitors have closed the gap in some key areas; that narrowing margin is encouraging the geopolitical tests Washington confronts today. There are questions regarding whether the United States still has enough military might to uphold key regional balances around the world, which are inseparable from questions about how wisely the country will address its long-term fiscal dilemmas. There are even graver questions as to whether Americans and their leaders still *want* to use the nation's power in the service of the postwar order. But the primary limiting factors here are political and psychological rather than material. They relate to historical amnesia, and to a reluctance to make hard choices and face hard facts, rather than any catastrophic collapse of American power. The United States still possesses advantages that most previous leading powers can only envy; its capabilities are surely sufficient—particularly when combined with the strengths of its allies—to mount a credible defense of the international system it has constructed. To say the U.S.-led order is endangered is a counsel of realism, but to say the situation is irretrievable is a counsel of unwarranted despair.

In fact, those who talk down America's geopolitical prospects and argue that the Pax Americana is doomed might consider whose geopolitical hand they would rather play, or what earlier period they would rather inhabit. Would they rather have the role of China—an impressive rising power, but one that is ringed by wary rivals and historical enemies, ruled by an authoritarian and increasingly personalist regime, and beset by looming economic, social, and demographic challenges? The role of Russia—a second-rate economic power whose geopolitical advances and daring stratagems have only masked the danger of long-term national decline? Would they rather face the situation America confronted in the early Cold War, when enemy tanks were stationed in the heart of Europe and there were power vacuums throughout the world's most critical regions? Or the situation in the mid-1970s, when the Kremlin was reaching for military primacy, there were fewer than forty democracies in the world, and capitalism seemed to be on the verge of collapse?

The threats today are compelling and urgent, and there may someday come a time when the balance of power has shifted so markedly that the postwar international system cannot be sustained. Yet that moment of failure has not yet arrived, and so the goal of U.S. strategy should be not to hasten it by giving up prematurely, but to push it off as far into the future as possible. Rather than simply acquiescing in the decline of a world it spent generations building, America should aggressively bolster its defenses, with an eye to preserving and perhaps even selectively advancing its remarkable achievements.

In 1947, the influential State Department official Charles Bohlen observed that the dream of collective security and universal cooperation was dead, killed off by an emerging Cold War. There was "complete disunity between the Soviet Union and the satellites on one side and the rest of the world on the other," he wrote. "There are, in short, two worlds instead of one." Yet this "disagreeable fact" was not cause for despair, because the free world could still hold its own if it closed ranks "politically, economically, financially, and, in the last analysis, militarily."[9] The United States and the other free nations, Bohlen understood, might not be able to attain the holy grail of a seamless, fully integrated global order. But they had the strength to defend and gradually expand a thriving liberal order covering large swaths of the world, so long as they could summon the resolve, cohesion, and will to use that strength effectively. It was a good description of the task in 1947, and one that seems little less apt today.

IV

Preserving a free and open order cannot be done on the cheap, however, nor can it be undertaken as a solitary effort. A fourth facet of a tragic sensibility is an understanding of the corresponding need for collective action and communal sacrifice. John F. Kennedy's inaugural address is most remembered for his promise that his generation of Americans, "tempered by war, disciplined by a hard and bitter peace," would "pay any price, bear any burden" in the service of a liberal world order. Yet Kennedy also believed that discord between allies or at home portended disaster, and so he warned that the defenders of that order "dare not meet a powerful challenge at odds and split asunder."[10] Today, one should not take Kennedy's counsel too literally: the United States and its allies cannot pay *any* price to promote their interests and values without depleting the resources and resolve needed to operate effectively in the world. The basic spirit of his admonition, however, remains relevant.

Amid the uniquely benign conditions of the post–Cold War era, it was all too easy for Americans to conclude that they would forever be able to enjoy the virtues of a steadily expanding liberal order while paying a steadily decreasing cost for the privilege. After all, in the 1990s America *could* have its military primacy on the cheap; the spread of democracy and markets *did* seem almost inexorable; it did not appear entirely unreasonable to think that geopolitical rivals *would* ultimately be tamed by the pacifying forces of globalization. The post–Cold War moment is indisputably over, however, so recovering a tragic mindset means dispensing with these pleasant but unsustainable expectations.

Americans must understand that favorable military balances undergird all the security, prosperity, and liberal progress to which they have become accustomed, and that maintaining those balances in a more competitive era will inevitably come at a higher price. They must understand, then, that the United States will have to make difficult fiscal trade-offs in the coming decades to sustain its global project.[11] They must understand that the United States will have to accept greater dangers and higher tensions to check the behavior of revisionist powers— that a willingness to risk conflict is sometimes the price of avoiding it. They must understand that the price of sustaining an open international economy is not zero, but that the price of not sustaining it, and thereby risking the tremendous prosperity that freer flows of trade and investment have delivered, is much higher. They must understand that protecting democratic values and human rights when they come under siege will require determination and persistent engagement. Above all, they must understand that the world will only be as congenial as they are willing to make it, and that if they decline to pay the costs and make the sacrifices involved in shaping the world, then they will also have to forfeit the benefits.

The "bitter truth," George Kennan remarked in 1947, was that "in this world you cannot even do good today unless you are prepared to exert your share of power, to take your share of responsibility, to make your share of mistakes, and to assume your share of risks."[12] The bitter truth today is that all Americans will have to contribute and risk more, in one way or another, if the world order from which they benefit so much is to endure— and that U.S. political leaders will have to ensure that both those sacrifices and the resulting benefits are widely shared.

What's true for America is equally true for its broader coalition of like-minded states. In geopolitics as in many things, there is great strength in numbers. Yet that strength will hold only if the supporters of the international order lock arms and commit fully to its defense. Preventing great-power war and international aggression, promoting an open global economy that averts depression and privation, upholding democracy and human rights in the face of authoritarian resurgence, and defending liberal norms that are being assaulted are goals that can be achieved only through strong partnerships and collective effort. If the democracies are divided, the autocracies will exploit those divisions; if America and its allies struggle to achieve unity of action, they will be outmaneuvered or overawed by revisionist powers. The trend in today's environment is, in many ways, toward greater fragmentation within what was once called the "free world." But a tragic mindset requires understanding that greater coordination and solidarity is required if that free world is to prosper.

For defenders of the international order, then, the question is not *whether* such coordination and solidarity is desirable, but *how* it can best be achieved. Here there is no escaping the centrality of American leadership. It is fair enough to point out that America pays a disproportionate share of the costs of sustaining an order that benefits so many. It is entirely reasonable, at a time when threats are rising and challenges multiplying, to demand that collective sacrifices be distributed more evenly, if only because Americans themselves will tire of supporting that order if they feel that they are doing it alone. To put the matter baldly, Americans will not be forever willing to send their sons and daughters to die for NATO if some of the richest countries in that alliance refuse to field minimally capable militaries of their own.

What Americans must remember, though, is that the strong collective measures required to preserve the international order are far more likely to emerge when America itself is fully committed. Allies and partners will be more willing to run risks and confront revisionist powers if they are assured of U.S. support than if they doubt it. An Asia-Pacific without American leadership would not be a region better positioned to resist Chinese expansionism; it would be a weaker and more divided region, increasingly at Beijing's mercy. Likewise, supporters of free markets and democracy are more likely to stand up for those arrangements if the world's preeminent free-market democracy is in the vanguard; collective action to meet

the greatest global challenges will materialize more successfully if the United States acts as the convener. America was "the
one nation that has the necessary political, military, and economic instruments at our disposal to catalyze a successful collective response," James Baker said during the Persian Gulf
crisis in 1990; no other nation can play this role, even today.[13]
Finally, Americans must keep in mind that if Washington pur-
sues protectionist economic policies that impoverish its partners, if it forsakes the liberal principles that have formed the
ideological core of its alliances, if it extorts tribute from its allies
like some mafia protection racket, then it will lose the attractive
power that allowed it to lead such formidable coalitions in the
first place. America endures its share of inequities and burdens
in the service of global order. Yet as a tragic sensibility reminds
us, some burdens are tolerable because they help prevent something far, far worse.

V

This leads to a fifth point, which is that a tragic sensibility grasps
the imperative of both timely and enduring action. Greek tragedy alerted its viewers to the storm clouds gathering over the
protagonists, as a way of reminding the spectators that their
circumstances were never quite as secure as they might appear,
and that averting disaster required acting to wrench events off
their tragic course. At a time when the trajectory of global affairs often seems so foreboding, cultivating a tragic sensibility
means being alert to the need to take early measures to stanch
the slow bleeding away of power, credibility, and ultimately
security.

　　This is important because much of today's revisionist
behavior represents conscious efforts to test the defenses of the

international order—to see which portions are strong and which invite challenge. "Probe with a bayonet," Lenin said: "If you meet steel, stop. If you meet mush, then push."[14] Such probes—whether the use of chemical weapons against civilian populations, attacks by Russian actors on democratic processes in Europe and the United States, or incremental Chinese expansionism in the South China Sea—also need to be understood as tests of credibility for the United States and its allies, regarding which positions and principles they will defend and which they will surrender. Credibility is, of course, impossible to measure. But given that the international system ultimately rests on America's perceived willingness to defend it, the loss of credibility matters enormously for friend and foe alike. As credibility dissipates, allies become less willing to count on the United States and the defenders of open society feel less secure. Sensing division and lack of resolve, aggressors become emboldened to push harder. "If the question is raised whether [credibility] is worth fighting over," Thomas Schelling observed, the answer is that it is "one of the few things worth fighting over."[15] It can be costly to take measures, whether diplomatic, economic, or military, to counter probing behavior early. But it can be costlier to delay until that behavior has acquired momentum and the credibility of those opposed to it has collapsed.

The same applies to vindicating norms and principles when they are attacked. The liberal international order does not reside on any map, but that does not mean it doesn't exist.[16] Concepts like freedom of navigation and nonaggression may seem abstract or remote; in reality, they are concrete and central, for they are the intellectual foundations on which peace and stability rest. What is at issue in the South China Sea, then, is not who controls a few "rocks and reefs," any more than the Korean War was about which dictator controlled Seoul or the

Persian Gulf War was about restoring the Kuwaiti royal family
to power. At issue is whether coercion will succeed in shifting
the status quo and undermining the international system. "It's
not the *thing* we object to," Winston Churchill remarked to a
woman who wondered why any Briton should care about Mussolini's invasion of Abyssinia, "It's the *kind* of thing."[17] As
Churchill understood, the survival of any international order
depends on whether its guiding principles are respected. And
failing to defend those principles the first time they are challenged—whether in Abyssinia or Manchuria in the 1930s, or in
Ukraine or the South China Sea today—virtually ensures that
escalating challenges will occur in the future. Here, too, a
tragic sensibility reminds us that waiting to confront destabilizing behavior may be the easiest course, but it is not necessarily
the wisest.

Finally, an understanding of tragedy underscores that
efforts to defend a particular international order permit no rest
and have no foreseeable end. There is nothing organic about a
world that promotes political liberty or economic openness.
There is no natural law that states that the American-led system,
for all its flaws, is guaranteed to endure simply because it is
more attractive than authoritarian alternatives. These arrangements have persisted only because they have rested on a foundation of power and persistent engagement. When either the
power or the engagement vanishes, so will the order it supports.

It may seem depressing to think that the United States is
condemned to eternal, arduous struggle—what the British
statesman Lord Vansittart described as "an endless game played
for joyless victory."[18] Yet those with a tragic sensibility know
better. On the ancient stage, acts of defiance and courage were
celebrated as heroic, precisely because they were acts of creation.
A tragic sensibility recognizes that there is similar heroism in

unceasing labors to stave off the forces of authoritarian resurgence and geopolitical decay.

VI

Those labors must, however, be tempered by a sense of proportion and restraint: this is the sixth imperative of a tragic sensibility. For the Greeks, hubris was no less a sin than complacency; excessive ambition was as dangerous as insufficient courage. America, too, has encountered trouble when it has succumbed to strategic indiscipline and the temptation to overuse or misuse its great power. Urgency and ambition are indispensable to any order-building project: how can any society undertake an endeavor so bold without them? Yet they must be carefully metered if they are not to lead to exhaustion and withdrawal.

This is not merely an abstract point, but one that is grounded in America's historical experience. The U.S. intervention in Vietnam not only failed to accomplish its immediate objectives, but ushered in a period of self-doubt and self-flagellation that hamstrung American policy through the 1970s, even as international dangers mounted. The current crisis of U.S. internationalism is, in the same way, at least partially the residue of what many Americans concluded was an excessively ambitious intervention in Iraq. There remain vibrant debates about the initial wisdom and ultimately winnability of both wars. What is indisputable is that when the United States is perceived by its own citizens to have gone too far or blundered into a quagmire, the resulting backlash inevitably undercuts even more prudent and necessary assertions of American power. "Strategies of 'maximalism' and 'retrenchment' bear an obvious cyclical relation to each other," writes Stephen Sestanovich: the excesses of the former lead directly to the dangers of the latter.[19]

This dynamic has several implications for U.S. strategy. It means recognizing that while the promotion of liberal values is important to U.S. national security, particularly in the context of a sharpening global ideological context, the use of force to catalyze political transformation in historically illiberal societies is an incredibly fraught proposition. It requires understanding that there are cases, such as a North Korean nuclear capability, where the tragedies involved in solving a problem decisively are probably greater than the tragedies involved in vigilantly managing it indefinitely. It entails acknowledging that even a superpower must pick its spots, emphasizing the most pressing issues—such as great-power competition—and treating others—such as terrorism—as economies of force. It means understanding that America may need to focus on preserving order and international stability in the short run—even if that requires distasteful cooperation with friendly authoritarian regimes such as Vietnam or Saudi Arabia—as the price of sustaining an international system in which liberty can flourish in the long run. Above all, it means accepting that the wages of hubris and hypervigilance are often disillusion and disengagement, and avoiding the twin dangers identified by Niebuhr at the outset of the postwar era. "Nations, as individuals, may be assailed by contradictory temptations," he wrote. "They may be tempted to flee the responsibilities of their power or refuse to develop their potentialities. But they may also refuse to recognize the limits of their possibilities and seek greater power than is given to mortals."[20]

There is, unfortunately, no mathematical formula for balancing assertiveness and restraint. There is no precise way of calculating the costs of action versus the costs of inaction, if only because the costs of inaction do not materialize when an active policy succeeds. And, of course, there is an inherent tension between seeking to shape the world and acknowledging the limits of one's ability to do so. This is why the United States, even during a period when it has generally been so constructively committed, has periodically oscillated between doing too much and doing too little. But one can, perhaps, hope that simply by realizing that tragedy lurks at both of these extremes, Americans may be marginally more skilled at steering between them.

VII

How, then, to inspire this sense of conviction, courage, and balance? How to re-instill in Americans the tragic sensibility they so urgently need? The challenge of doing all this in many ways boils down to the challenge of convincing democratic societies to act before it is too late, and of reminding them of what they are fighting to preserve—and avoid—in the first place. The liberal international order is built upon a positive agenda that has promoted great wealth and well-being. Yet it is also predicated upon preventing another plunge back into the abyss. And just as the most successful international orders looked backward as well as forward, an engagement with history offers the best way of recapturing a tragic sensibility without having to experience tragedy in the flesh.

In ancient Athens, tragedies used distant, mythical history to illuminate contemporary challenges. Today, we need not look back to an imagined past. Recovering a tragic sensibility means only re-familiarizing ourselves with a history that is so edifying precisely because it is so real.

By understanding the frequency with which prosperous and seemingly stable worlds have plunged into darkness, we can better appreciate the inherent fallibility of our own creations. By revisiting the painstaking efforts that were required to build and sustain international order in the past, we might better grasp the labors that remain necessary to perpetuate the American-led order. By returning to the creation of the postwar system in the years after 1945, we can remind ourselves why the United States does so many extraordinary things—leading the international economy, patrolling distant borders, anchoring military alliances around the globe—whose rationales now seem so abstract and difficult to explain. And by reacquainting ourselves with all this history, we can reteach ourselves the lesson that previous generations of statesmen instinctively understood—that the alternative to modest sacrifices today is likely to be the necessity of making much larger and more painful sacrifices later. "Fools learn by experience, wise men learn by others' experience," Otto von Bismarck once said. Today, Americans could benefit enormously from the sort of vicarious experience history has to offer.[21]

For in the final analysis, the key geopolitical questions confronting the United States and the international order it created are not simply questions of power. They are equally questions of perception and willpower.[22] Will the countries that have historically defended the international order summon the nerve and unity to defend it again today? Will they realize that it is not historical inevitability, or some triumph of moral progress, but rather incessant and determined effort that holds geopolitical disasters at bay? Will they remember precisely how bad things can get, and how quickly they can get that way, when international orders fall apart? Will they overcome the naïve ahistoricism that risks blinding them to these realities? The United States and its allies once found, in tragedy, the determination necessary to create something imperfect but beautiful. Will they now recover an equivalent determination to keep that good thing going?

The Greeks understood the challenge of maintaining a tragic sensibility over time, which is why they enshrined tragedy as the central, and most visible, part of their culture. They did so to cultivate a political culture that was both sober and optimistic, believing that optimism without sobriety led to hubris and overreach, and that sobriety without optimism led to paralysis in the face of danger. For them, as for older generations of Americans, the past served as a source of both terror and inspiration.

Today, it is impractical for whole societies to cram themselves into the narrow benches of a theater. But without a similar determination to recover a history that Americans now seem determined to forget, we will surely squander something essential. In writing about the successes and ultimate failure of the Concert of Europe in the nineteenth century, Henry Kissinger observed that "in the long interval of peace the sense of the tragic was lost; it was forgotten that states could die, that upheavals could be irretrievable."[23] One suspects that Americans will soon end up relearning these lessons one way or another. They will do so either by reacquainting themselves with a tragic sensibility, or by experiencing the real-world tragedy that their amnesia, if not corrected, may help bring about.

Notes

Introduction

1. Robert F. Kennedy, "Statement on Assassination of Martin Luther King, Jr.," Indianapolis, April 4, 1968, https://www.jfklibrary.org/Research/Research-Aids/Ready-Reference/RFK-Speeches/Statement-on-the-Assassination-of-Martin-Luther-King.aspx.

2. Evan Thomas, *Robert Kennedy: His Life* (New York: Simon and Schuster, 2002), 285–287; Edith Hamilton, *The Greek Way* (New York: Norton, 1942).

3. Aristotle, *Poetics*, 1451a, in Richard McKeon, ed., *The Basic Works of Aristotle* (New York: Random House, 1941), 1463.

4. Larry Bland, Mark Stoler, Sharon Ritenour Stevens, and Daniel Holt, eds., *The Papers of George Catlett Marshall*, vol. 6 (Baltimore: Johns Hopkins University Press, 2013), 49.

5. Donald Kagan, *On the Origins of War and the Preservation of Peace* (New York: Anchor Books, 1996), 566.

6. Ralph Waldo Emerson, *The Prose Works of Ralph Waldo Emerson, In Two Volumes,* vol. 2 (Boston: Fields, Osgood, & Co., 1870), 318.

1

The Virtues of Tragedy

1. Thucydides, *The Landmark Thucydides: A Comprehensive Guide to the Peloponnesian War,* ed. Robert B. Strassler (New York: Simon & Schuster, 1996), Book I, Paragraph 70. Hereafter, Thucydides, *Landmark Thucydides,* followed by the book and paragraph numbers standard in all editions.

2. Thucydides, *Landmark Thucydides,* II.41.

3. Edith Hamilton, *The Greek Way* (New York: Norton, 1942), 227.

4. Aristophanes, *Frogs,* in Jeffrey Henderson, trans., *Aristophanes: Frogs, Assemblymen, Wealth* (Cambridge, MA: Harvard University Press, 2002), 161.

5. Friedrich Nietzsche, *The Birth of Tragedy: Out of the Spirit of Music* (1872; London: Penguin Books, 2003), 3.

6. Aristotle, *On Rhetoric,* 1391b, trans. George Kennedy (Oxford: Oxford University Press, 2007), 155.

7. Aristotle, *On Rhetoric,* 1383a, in Kennedy translation, 130.

8. Hamilton, *The Greek Way,* 244. See also Bryan Doerries, *The Theater of War: What Ancient Greek Tragedies Can Teach Us Today* (New York: Alfred A. Knopf, 2015), 23.

9. John Lewis Gaddis, *On Grand Strategy* (New York: Penguin, 2018), esp. 170.

10. Nietzsche, *The Birth of Tragedy,* 100.

11. Herodotus, *The Landmark Herodotus: The Histories,* ed. Robert B. Strassler (New York: Random House, 2007), 523.

12. Aeschylus, *The Persians,* in *Prometheus Bound and Other Plays,* trans. Philip Vellacott (London: Penguin, 1961), 142.

13. Aeschylus, *Persians,* 144, 145, 150.

14. Euripides, *Iphigenia at Aulis,* trans. George Theodoridis, http://www.poetryintranslation.com/PITBR/Greek/Iphigeneia.php.

15. Euripides, *Iphigenia at Aulis.*

16. Euripides, *The Heracleidae,* in *Euripides,* vol. 3, trans. David Grene and Richard Lattimore (Chicago: University of Chicago Press, 1959), 127.

17. Euripides, *The Suppliant Women,* quoted in Donald Kagan, ed., *Sources in Greek Political Thought: From Homer to Polybius* (New York: Free Press, 1965), 132.

18. Aeschylus, *The Eumenides,* in *The Oresteia,* trans. David Grene and Wendy Doniger O'Flaherty (Chicago: University of Chicago Press, 1989), 160.

19. Thucydides, *Landmark Thucydides,* II.41.

20. Thucydides, *Landmark Thucydides,* II.42.

21. Thucydides, *Landmark Thucydides,* II.43.

22. Thucydides, *Landmark Thucydides,* II.53.

23. Thucydides, *Landmark Thucydides,* II.61.

24. Thucydides, *Landmark Thucydides,* I.22.

2
Tragedy as the Norm

1. Steven Pinker, *Better Angels of Our Nature: Why Violence Has Declined* (New York: Viking, 2011).

2. George H. W. Bush, "Address Before a Joint Session of the Congress on the Persian Gulf Crisis and the Federal Budget Deficit," September 11, 1990, American Presidency Project (APP), http://www.presidency.ucsb.edu/.

3. Robert Jervis, "Theories of War in an Era of Leading-Power Peace," *American Political Science Review* 91, no. 2 (2002): 1.

4. *The National Security of the United States of America*, September 2002, https://www.state.gov/documents/organization/63562.pdf.

5. Francis Fukuyama, "The End of History?" *National Interest* 16 (1989): 18.

6. John Mearsheimer, *The Tragedy of Great Power Politics* (New York: Norton, 2014), 2.

7. Paul Kennedy, *Rise and Fall of the Great Powers* (New York: Vintage, 1988).

8. Thomas Hobbes, *Leviathan: Or the Matter, Forme and Power of a Commonwealth Ecclesiasticall and Civil*, ed. Michael Oakeshott (New York: Simon & Schuster, 1962), 94.

9. On the war and its causes, see Donald Kagan, *The Outbreak of the Peloponnesian War* (Ithaca, NY: Cornell University Press, 1969); Victor Davis Hanson, *A War Like No Other: How the Athenians and Spartans Fought the Peloponnesian War* (New York: Random House, 2005); Jennifer Roberts, *The Plague of War: Athens, Sparta, and the Struggle for Ancient Greece* (New York: Oxford University Press, 2017).

10. Thucydides, *Landmark Thucydides*, III.82; I.1.

11. Thucydides, *Landmark Thucydides*, I.23.

12. Thucydides, *Landmark Thucydides*, III.81; also Donald Kagan, *The Fall of the Athenian Empire* (Ithaca, NY: Cornell University Press, 1991), 411–417.

13. Thucydides, *Landmark Thucydides*, V.89; III.82.

14. Thucydides, *Landmark Thucydides*, I.22.

15. Geoffrey Blainey, *The Causes of War* (New York: Free Press, 1988), 3.

16. Michael Howard, *The Invention of Peace and the Reinvention of War* (New Haven: Yale University Press, 2001), 12–13.

17. Geoffrey Parker, ed., *The Thirty Years' War* (New York: Routledge, 1997), 12.

18. Parker, *Thirty Years' War*, 11; Brendan Simms, *Europe: The Struggle for Supremacy, from 1453 to the Present* (New York: Basic Books, 2013), 10–37; Myron Guttman, "The Origins of the Thirty Years' War," *Journal of Interdisciplinary History* 18, no. 4 (1988): 749–770.

19. On the range of estimates, see Peter Wilson, *The Thirty Years' War: Europe's Tragedy* (Cambridge, MA: Harvard University Press, 2009), esp. 787.

20. Geoff Mortimer, *Eyewitness Accounts of the Thirty Years' War* (New York: Palgrave, 2002), 69–70.

21. Parker, *Thirty Years' War*, 179.

22. The origins and achievements of both the Peace of Westphalia and the Concert of Europe are discussed at greater length in the next chapter.

23. James Sheehan, *Where Have All the Soldiers Gone? The Transformation of Modern Europe* (New York: Mariner, 2008), xviii.

24. Thomas Pangle and Peter Ahrensdorft, *Justice Among Nations: On the Moral Basis of Power and Peace* (Lawrence: University of Kansas Press, 1999), 159–160.

25. Immanuel Kant, "Perpetual Peace: A Philosophical Sketch," in Kant, *Perpetual Peace and Other Essays,* trans. Ted Humphrey (Indianapolis: Hackett, 1983).

26. Williamson Murray, *America and the Future of War: The Past as Prologue* (Stanford, CA: Hoover Institution Press, 2016), 7; also Pinker, *Better Angels of Our Nature,* 161–166; David Bell, *The First Total War: Napoleon's Europe and the Birth of Warfare as We Know It* (New York: Mariner, 2007), 1–2, 63–78.

27. Bell, *First Total War,* 115; also Stephen Walt, *Revolution and War* (Ithaca, NY: Cornell University Press, 1996).

28. Bell, *First Total War,* 2–3.

29. Bell, *First Total War,* 7.

30. Carl von Clausewitz, *On War,* ed. and trans. Michael Howard and Peter Paret (Princeton, NJ: Princeton University Press, 1984), 592–593.

31. Mike Rapport, *The Napoleonic Wars: A Very Short Introduction* (New York: Oxford University Press, 2013), 1.

32. Bell, *First Total War,* 3.

33. Norman Angell, *The Great Illusion: A Study of the Relation of Military Power in Nations to Their Economic and Social Advantage* (London: W. Heinemann, 1911). See also Margaret MacMillan, *The War That Ended Peace: How Europe Abandoned Peace for the First World War* (London: Profile Books, 2014), xxiii–xxv.

34. Sheehan, *Where Have All The Soldiers Gone?* 22.

35. MacMillan, *The War That Ended Peace,* 593; Christopher Clark, *The Sleepwalkers: How Europe Went to War in 1914* (New York: Harper Perennial, 2014).

36. Alfred Havighurst, *Britain in Transition: The Twentieth Century* (Chicago: University of Chicago Press, 1985), 125.

37. Niall Ferguson, *The Pity of War* (London: Penguin, 1999), 210.

38. Sheehan, *Where Have All the Soldiers Gone?* 99.

39. Adam Tooze, *The Deluge: The Great War, America, and the Remaking of the Global Order, 1916–1931* (New York: Penguin, 2014), 3.

40. The best account remains Gerhard Weinberg, *A World at Arms: A Global History of World War II* (New York: Cambridge University Press, 1994).

41. Donald Kagan, *On the Origins of War and the Preservation of Peace* (New York: Anchor Books, 1996), 331. For a fuller treatment of Churchill's interwar views, see John Maurer, " 'Winston Has Gone Mad': Churchill, the British Admiralty, and the Rise of Japanese Naval Power," *Journal of Strategic Studies* 35, no. 6 (2012): 775–798.

42. E. H. Carr, *The Twenty Years' Crisis, 1919–1939: An Introduction to the Study of International Relations* (New York: St. Martin's, 1946), 36.

43. Kagan, *On the Origins of War and the Preservation of Peace*, 405.

44. Sheehan, *Where Have All the Soldiers Gone?* 122.

45. *Survey of International Affairs* (London: Oxford University Press, 1932), 189.

46. See Richard Frank, *Downfall: The End of the Imperial Japanese Empire* (New York: Penguin, 1999).

47. Paul Fussell, *The Great War and Modern Memory: The Illustrated Edition* (New York: Sterling, 2009), 7.

3
Tragedy as Inspiration

1. Plato, *Menexenus*, 236d, in Malcolm Schofield, ed., *Plato: Gorgias, Menexenus, Protagoras* (Cambridge: Cambridge University Press, 2010), 120.

2. Oliver Wendell Holmes Jr., Memorial Day Address, May 30, 1884, http://www.people.virginia.edu/~mmd5f/memorial.htm.

3. G. John Ikenberry, *After Victory: Institutions, Strategic Restraint, and the Rebuilding of Order After Major Wars* (Princeton, NJ: Princeton University Press, 2001), 3.

4. Henry Kissinger, *Diplomacy* (New York: Simon & Schuster, 1994), 61.

5. C. V. Wedgwood, *The Thirty Years' War* (London: Jonathan Cape, 1964), 513; David Blaney and Naeem Inayatullah, "The Westphalian Deferral," *International Studies Review* 2, no. 2 (2000): 29–64.

6. Benjamin Straumann, "The Peace of Westphalia as a Secular Constitution," *Constellations* 15, no. 2 (2008): 179.

7. Derek Croxton, "The Peace of Westphalia of 1648 and the Origins of Sovereignty," *International History Review* 21, no. 3 (1999): 589.

8. Wedgwood, *Thirty Years' War*, 526.

9. Hugo Grotius, *The Law of War and Peace (De jure belli ac pacis): A New Translation*, trans. Louise Ropes Loomis (Roslyn, NY: Walter J. Black, 1949), 10, 433; Charles Hill, *Grand Strategies: Literature, Statecraft, and World Order* (New Haven: Yale University Press, 2010), 73–79.

10. Garrett Mattingly, *Renaissance Diplomacy* (Baltimore: Penguin, 1964).

11. Alfred van Staden, *Between the Rule of Power and the Power of Rule: In Search of an Effective World Order* (Boston: Martinus Nijhoff, 2007), 21.

12. Geoffrey Parker, ed., *The Thirty Years' War* (New York: Routledge, 1997), 195.

13. Robert and Isabelle Tombs, *That Sweet Enemy: The French and the British from the Sun King to the Present* (New York: Knopf, 2007), 44.

14. Brendan Simms, Michael Axworthy, and Patrick Milton, "Ending the New Thirty Years War," *New Statesman,* January 26, 2016, https://www.newstatesman.com/politics/uk/2016/01/ending-new-thirty-years-war.

15. Michael Howard, *War in European History* (New York: Oxford University Press, 2009), 63–72.

16. Memorandum of Lord Castlereagh, August 12, 1815, in C. K. Webster, ed., *British Diplomacy, 1813–1815: Select Documents Dealing with the Reconstruction of Europe* (London: G. Bell and Sons, 1921), 361–362.

17. Asa Briggs and Patricia Clavin, *Modern Europe, 1789–Present* (New York: Routledge, 2013), 44.

18. Paul Schroeder, "Did the Vienna Settlement Rest upon a Balance of Power?" *American Historical Review* 97 (1992): 687–706.

19. Harold Nicolson, *The Congress of Vienna: A Study in Allied Unity, 1812–1822* (New York: Harcourt, 1946), 155.

20. Ikenberry, *After Victory,* 91; Robert Jervis, "From Balance to Concert: A Study of International Security Cooperation," *World Politics* 38, no. 1 (1985), esp. 59.

21. Philip Bobbitt, *The Shield of Achilles: War, Peace, and the Course of History* (New York: Knopf, 2002), 164.

22. Brendan Simms, *Europe: The Struggle for Supremacy, from 1453 to the Present* (New York: Basic Books, 2013), 178.

23. Gordon A. Craig and Alexander L. George, *Force and Statecraft: Diplomatic Problems of Our Time* (New York: Oxford University Press, 1995), 28.

24. *Correspondence, Despatches, and Other Papers of Viscount Castlereagh, Second Marquess of Londonderry,* 2nd ser., vol. 8 (London: William Shoberl, 1851), 356.

25. Henry A. Kissinger, *A World Restored: Metternich, Castlereagh, and the Problems of Peace, 1812–1822* (Boston: Houghton Mifflin, 1973), 318.

26. Paul Schroeder, "The 19th-Century International System: Changes in the Structure," *World Politics* 39, no. 1 (1986): 3.

27. See Erez Manela, *The Wilsonian Moment: Self-Determination and the International Origins of Anticolonial Nationalism* (New York: Oxford University Press, 2007).

28. Woodrow Wilson, Address to a Joint Session of Congress Requesting a Declaration of War Against Germany, April 2, 1917, APP.

29. "President Wilson's Fourteen Points," Delivered in Joint Session, January 8, 1918, APP.

30. Woodrow Wilson, Address to the Senate of the United States: "A World League for Peace," January 22, 1917, APP.

31. Lloyd Ambrosius, *Woodrow Wilson and the American Diplomatic Tradition: The Treaty Fight in Perspective* (New York: Cambridge University Press, 1990), 78; Henry Kissinger, *Diplomacy* (New York: Simon & Schuster, 1994), 52.

32. John Milton Cooper, *Breaking the Heart of the World: Woodrow Wilson and the Fight for the League of Nations* (New York: Cambridge University Press, 2001), 158.

33. Donald Kagan, *On the Origins of War and the Preservation of Peace* (New York: Anchor Books, 1996), 304.

34. "Address to the Senate on the Versailles Peace Treaty," July 10, 1919, APP.

35. For various perspectives on the peace treaty, see Harold Nicholson, *Peacemaking, 1919* (London: Grosset and Dunlap, 1933); Margaret MacMillan, *Paris 1919: Six Months That Changed the World* (New York: Random House, 2002); Sally Marks, *Illusion of Peace: International Relations in Europe, 1918–1933* (London: Macmillan, 1976).

36. Richard Overy, *The Road to War* (London: Penguin, 1999), 122.

37. On the treaty fight, see Cooper, *Breaking the Heart of the World*.

38. Oona Hathaway and Scott Shapiro, *The Internationalists: How a Radical Plan to Outlaw War Remade the World* (New York: Simon & Schuster, 2017), 129.

39. George F. Kennan, *Memoirs, 1950–1963* (Boston: Little, Brown, 1972), 71.

40. Andreas Hillgruber, *Germany and the Two World Wars* (Cambridge, MA: Harvard University Press, 1982), 56–57.

41. Paul Kennedy, *The Rise and Fall of British Naval Mastery* (London: Ashfield, 1986), 271–272.

42. Hugh Ragsdale, *The Soviets, the Munich Crisis, and the Coming of World War II* (New York: Cambridge University Press, 2004), 3; Williamson Murray, "British Grand Strategy, 1933–1942," in Williamson Murray, Richard Hart Sinnreich, and James Lacey, eds., *The Shaping of Grand Strategy: Policy, Diplomacy, and War* (Cambridge: Cambridge University Press, 2011), 150–151.

43. Ronald Steel, *Walter Lippmann and the American Century* (Boston: Little, Brown, 1980), 156.

44. Lynne Olson, *Those Angry Days: Roosevelt, Lindbergh, and America's Fight over World War II, 1939–1941* (New York: Random House, 2013), 28.

45. David Lloyd George, *War Memoirs*, vol. 1 (London: Odhams, 1938), 49.

46. Richard Overy, *The Twilight Years: The Paradox of Britain Between the Wars* (New York: Viking, 2009), 176.

47. Ernest Hemingway, "Notes on the Next War: A Serious Topical Letter," *Esquire*, September 1935, 156.

48. Murray, "British Grand Strategy, 1933–1942," 157; also Corelli Barnett, *The Collapse of British Power* (London: William Morrow, 1972).

49. Telford Taylor, *Munich: The Price of Peace* (Garden City, NY: Doubleday, 1979), 884.

50. Kagan, *On the Origins of War and the Preservation of Peace*, 567.

4

The Great Escape

1. Quotes from John Mueller, "Quiet Cataclysm: Some Afterthoughts on World War III," in Michael J. Hogan, ed., *The End of the Cold War: Its Meaning and Implications* (New York: Cambridge University Press, 1992), 43; also Mueller, *Retreat from Doomsday: The Obsolescence of Major War* (New York: Basic Books, 1989), 97, 98, 109.

2. Arnold Toynbee, *War and Civilization* (New York: Oxford University Press, 1950), 4.

3. Robert Jervis, "The Political Effects of Nuclear Weapons: A Comment," *International Security* 13, no. 2 (1988): 80.

4. Eric Hobsbawm, *The Age of Extremes: A History of the World, 1914–1991* (New York: Vintage, 1996).

5. Hobsbawm, *Age of Extremes*, 271.

6. Paul Kennedy, *The Rise and Fall of the Great Powers* (New York: Vintage, 1988), 369; G. John Ikenberry, *After Victory: Institutions, Strategic Restraint, and the Rebuilding of Order After Major Wars* (Princeton, NJ: Princeton University Press, 2001), 168.

7. Henry Luce, "The American Century," *Life*, February 17, 1941.

8. Truman, "Remarks in Chicago at the Shriners Diamond Jubilee Banquet," July 19, 1949, APP.

9. Walter Isaacson and Evan Thomas, *The Wise Men: Six Friends and the World They Made* (New York: Simon & Schuster, 1986).

10. Greg Behrman, *The Most Noble Adventure: The Marshall Plan and the Time When America Helped Save Europe* (New York: Free Press, 2007), 48.

11. John Fousek, *To Lead the Free World: American Nationalism and the Cultural Roots of the Cold War* (Chapel Hill: University of North Carolina Press, 2000), 53.

12. Hal Brands, *What Good Is Grand Strategy? Power and Purpose in American Statecraft from Harry S. Truman to George W. Bush* (Ithaca, NY: Cornell University Press, 2014), 19.

13. Truman, "Radio Report to the American People on the Potsdam Conference," August 9, 1945, APP.

14. Office of Strategic Services (OSS), "Problems and Objectives of United States Policy," April 12, 1945, Declassified Documents Reference System (DDRS); William Wohlforth, *The Elusive Balance: Power and Perceptions During the Cold War* (Ithaca, NY: Cornell University Press, 1993), 121–122.

15. Roosevelt, "Address at University of Virginia," June 10, 1940, APP.

16. George Herring, *From Colony to Superpower: U.S. Foreign Relations Since 1776* (New York: Oxford University Press, 2008), 598; also Melvyn Leffler, *A Preponderance of Power: National Security, the Truman Administration, and the Cold War* (Stanford, CA: Stanford University Press, 1992).

17. Benn Steil, *The Battle of Bretton Woods: John Maynard Keynes, Harry Dexter White, and the Making of a New World Order* (Princeton, NJ: Princeton University Press, 2013), 13.

18. Behrman, *Most Noble Adventure*, 48.

19. Douglas Irwin, *Clashing over Commerce: A History of U.S. Trade Policy* (Chicago: University of Chicago Press, 2017), 484.

20. Truman, "Address on Foreign Economic Policy, Delivered at Baylor University," March 6, 1947, APP.

21. See Barry Eichengreen, *Exorbitant Privilege: The Rise and Fall of the Dollar and the Future of the International Monetary System* (New York: Oxford University Press, 2011).

22. G. John Ikenberry, *Liberal Leviathan: The Origins, Crisis, and Transformation of the American World Order* (Princeton, NJ: Princeton University Press, 2011), 199.

23. Francis Gavin, *Gold, Dollars, and Power: The Politics of International Monetary Relations, 1958–1971* (Chapel Hill: University of North Carolina Press, 2004), 86.

24. Hobsbawm, *Age of Extremes,* 261; Tony Judt, *Postwar: A History of Europe Since 1945* (New York: Penguin, 2005), 91–99.

25. Dean Acheson, "The Requirements of Reconstruction," speech before the Delta Council, May 8, 1947, https://www.trumanlibrary.org/exhibit_documents/index.php?tldate=1947-05-05%20&groupid=3438&pagenumber=1&collectionid=marshallplan.

26. Michael Mastanduno, "System Maker and Privilege Taker: U.S. Power and the International Political Economy," *World Politics* 61, no. 1 (2009): 121–154.

27. Leffler, *Preponderance of Power,* esp. 160–164.

28. Truman, "Address on Foreign Economic Policy, Delivered at Baylor University."

29. Charles Mee, *The Marshall Plan* (New York: Simon & Schuster, 1985), 239.

30. "A Report to the National Security Council by the Executive Secretary on United States Objectives and Programs for National Security," NSC 68, April 14, 1950, http://fas.org/irp/offdocs/nsc-hst/nsc-68.htm; John Lewis Gaddis, *Strategies of Containment: A Critical Appraisal of Postwar American National Security Policy During the Cold War* (New York: Oxford University Press, 2005), 393; Aaron Friedberg, *In the Shadow of the Garrison State: America's Anti-Statism and Its Cold War Grand Strategy* (Princeton, NJ: Princeton University Press, 2000), 341.

31. Dean Acheson, *Present at the Creation: My Years in the State Department* (New York: Norton, 1987), 378.

32. Truman, "Special Message to the Congress on Greece and Turkey: The Truman Doctrine," March 12, 1947, APP.

33. Quoted in Walter McDougall, *Promised Land, Crusader State: The American Encounter with the World Since 1776* (Boston: Houghton Mifflin, 1997), 153.

34. Harry S. Truman, *Years of Trial and Hope* (Garden City, NJ: Doubleday, 1956), 332–333.

35. Roosevelt, "Address to the International Student Assembly," September 3, 1942, APP.

36. Ikenberry, *Liberal Leviathan.*

37. Dulles to Harold Macmillan, December 10, 1955, *Foreign Relations of the United States, 1955–1957,* vol. 4 (Washington, DC: U.S. Government Printing Office, 1988), 363.

38. Philip Jessup, *The Birth of Nations* (New York: Columbia University Press, 1974), 10.

39. Roosevelt, "Address at Hyde Park, New York," July 4, 1941, APP.

40. Sean Kay, *NATO and the Future of European Security* (Lanham, MD: Rowman & Littlefield, 1998), 30; also Tony Smith, *America's Mission: The United States and the Worldwide Struggle for Democracy in the Twentieth Century* (Princeton, NJ: Princeton University Press, 1994), esp. 111–176.

41. On U.S. democracy promotion efforts in the late Cold War, see Elliott Abrams, *Realism and Democracy: American Foreign Policy After the Arab Spring* (New York: Cambridge University Press, 2017), 1–91; Hal Brands, *Making the Unipolar Moment: U.S. Foreign Policy and the Rise of the Post–Cold War Order* (Ithaca, NY: Cornell University Press 2016), 119–171.

42. Truman, "Special Message to the Congress on Greece and Turkey."

43. John Lewis Gaddis, *The Long Peace: Inquiries into the History of the Cold War* (New York: Oxford University Press, 1986), 61.

44. Geir Lundestad, "Empire by Invitation? The United States and Western Europe, 1945–1952," *Journal of Peace Research* 23, no. 3 (1986): 263–277; John Lewis Gaddis, *We Now Know: Rethinking Cold War History* (New York: Oxford University Press, 1997).

45. Kennedy, "Inaugural Address," January 20, 1961, APP.

46. Isaacson and Thomas, *The Wise Men*, 368.

47. Francis Gavin, *Nuclear Statecraft: History and Strategy in America's Atomic Age* (Ithaca, NY: Cornell University Press, 2012), 57.

48. Michael Lind, *The American Way of Strategy: U.S. Foreign Policy and the American Way of Life* (New York: Oxford University Press, 2006), 107.

49. Kennan, "Planning of Foreign Policy," Lecture at the National War College, June 18, 1947, Box 298, George F. Kennan Papers, Seeley Mudd Manuscript Library, Princeton University.

50. David Reynolds, *From World War to Cold War: Churchill, Roosevelt, and the International History of the 1940s* (New York: Oxford University Press, 2006), 317.

51. Marc Trachtenberg, *A Constructed Peace: The Making of the European Settlement, 1945–1963* (Princeton, NJ: Princeton University Press, 1999), 147.

52. Isaiah Berlin, *The Hedgehog and the Fox: An Essay on Tolstoy's View of History* (New York: Simon & Schuster, 1953), 1. See also John Lewis Gaddis, *On Grand Strategy* (New York: Penguin, 2018), 3–27.

53. Walter Lippmann, *The Cold War: A Study in U.S. Foreign Policy* (New York: Harper & Brothers, 1947).

54. John Lewis Gaddis, *The Cold War* (London: Allen Lane, 2005), 165.

55. Acheson, *Present at the Creation*, 375.

56. "The Chargé in the Soviet Union (Kennan) to the Secretary of State," February 22, 1946, available at https://nsarchive2.gwu.edu//coldwar/documents/episode-1/kennan.htm.

57. Johnson, "Address at Johns Hopkins University: 'Peace Without Conquest,'" April 7, 1965, APP.

58. The "breathing space" argument is made in Mark Moyar, *Triumph Forsaken: The Vietnam War, 1954–1965* (New York: Cambridge University Press, 2006).

59. Henry Kissinger, *White House Years* (Boston: Little, Brown, 1979), 64.

60. Samuel Huntington, *The Third Wave: Democratization in the Late Twentieth Century* (Norman: University of Oklahoma Press, 1991), 26; Freedom House, *Freedom in the World 2013: Democratic Breakthroughs in the Balance,*

29, available at https://freedomhouse.org/sites/default/files/FIW%202013%20
Booklet.pdf.

61. World Trade Organization, *World Trade Report 2008: Trade in a Glo-balizing World*, 15, available at https://www.wto.org/english/res_e/booksp_e/
anrep_e/world_trade_report08_e.pdf.

62. Robert Kagan, *The World America Made* (New York: Vintage, 2012),
40–41.

63. The one potential exception would be the Korean War, in which the
United States and China fought each other. By most conventional definitions,
however, China did not qualify as a great power in 1950.

64. Mark Zacher, "The Territorial Integrity Norm: International Boundar-ies and the Use of Force," *International Organization* 55, no. 2 (2001): 215–250;
Steven Pinker, *Better Angels of Our Nature: Why Violence Has Declined* (New
York: Viking, 2011), 251.

65. Gaddis, *The Long Peace*.

66. Pinker, *Better Angels of Our Nature*; Oona Hathaway and Scott Shapiro,
The Internationalists: How a Radical Plan to Outlaw War Remade the World
(New York: Simon & Schuster, 2017).

67. As Lawrence Freedman has rightly noted, even nuclear weapons
only played their stabilizing role because the United States was willing to
threaten nuclear war not just on behalf of its own security but on behalf
of the security of its allies around the world. It was, he writes, America's
"alliance system that was considered to be the main deterrent, and thus the
best reason for Moscow not to consider aggression." Freedman, "Stephen
Pinker and the Long Peace: Alliance, Deterrence, and Decline," *Cold War
History* 14, no. 4 (2014): 667.

68. Truman, "The President's Farewell Address to the American People,"
January 15, 1953, APP.

69. George Orwell, *1984* (New York: Harcourt Brace, 1949), 267.

70. Hans Morgenthau, "The Mainsprings of American Foreign Policy: The
National Interest vs. Moral Abstractions," *American Political Science Review*
44, no. 4 (1950): 838.

5
The Contemporary Amnesia

1. Reinhold Niebuhr, *The Irony of American History* (New York: Charles
Scribner and Sons, 1952), 1.

2. *National Security Strategy of the United States* (Washington, DC: U.S.
Government Printing Office, 1990), 2; Hal Brands, *Making the Unipolar*

Moment: U.S. Foreign Policy and the Rise of the Post–Cold War Order (Ithaca, NY: Cornell University Press, 2016), 317–336, 347–360.

3. Baker, "Summons to Leadership," April 2, 1992, Box 169, James A. Baker III Papers, Princeton University.

4. George Bush and Brent Scowcroft, *A World Transformed* (New York: Vintage, 1999), 566.

5. Scowcroft to Bush, December 22, 1989, Box 10, OA/ID 91116, Chronological Files, German Unification Files, Brent Scowcroft Collection, George H. W. Bush Presidential Library. See also Jeffrey A. Engel, *When the World Seemed New: George H. W. Bush and the End of the Cold War* (Boston: Houghton Mifflin Harcourt, 2017).

6. Presidential Remarks to Congressional Leaders, undated (1990), Box 43, FOIA 1998-0099-F, George H. W. Bush Presidential Library; Bush, "Address Before a Joint Session of the Congress on the Persian Gulf Crisis and the Federal Budget Deficit," September 11, 1990, APP.

7. Patrick Tyler, "U.S. Strategy Plan Calls for Insuring No Rivals Develop," *New York Times*, March 8, 1992.

8. "To Paris, U.S. Looks Like a 'Hyperpower,'" *International Herald Tribune*, February 5, 1999.

9. Samuel Huntington, "The Lonely Superpower," *Foreign Affairs* 78, no. 2 (1999): 43.

10. John Mearsheimer, "Why We Will Soon Miss the Cold War," *Atlantic Monthly*, August 1990, 35–50.

11. William Wohlforth, "The Stability of a Unipolar World," *International Security* 24, no. 1 (1999), esp. 7.

12. See Stephen Brooks and William Wohlforth, *America Abroad: The United States' Global Role in the Twenty-First Century* (New York: Oxford University Press, 2016); Freedom House, *Freedom in the World 2013: Democratic Breakthroughs in the Balance,* 29, available at https://freedomhouse.org/sites/default/files/FIW%202013%20Booklet.pdf.

13. Robert Kagan, "The Benevolent Empire," *Foreign Policy* 111 (1998): 25; Zachary Selden, "Balancing Against or Balancing With? The Spectrum of Alignment and the Endurance of American Hegemony," *Security Studies* 22, no. 3 (2013): 330–363.

14. John Mearsheimer, "Why Is Europe Peaceful Today?" *European Political Science* 9, no. 3 (2010): 387–397, esp. 388.

15. David Halberstam, *War in a Time of Peace: Bush, Clinton, and the Generals* (New York: Scribner, 2001), 57–58.

16. Eric Nordlinger, *Isolationism Reconfigured: American Foreign Policy for a New Century* (Princeton, NJ: Princeton University Press, 1996), 18–19.

17. Patrick Tyler, "Halving Defense Budget in Decade Suggested," *Washington Post*, November 21, 1989.

18. Jeane Kirkpatrick, "A Normal Country in a Normal Time," *National Interest* 21 (1990): 40–44.

19. Patrick Buchanan, "America First—and Second, and Third," *National Interest* 19 (1990): 77–82.

20. See the military expenditures database maintained by the Stockholm International Peace Research Institute, https://www.sipri.org/sites/default/files/Milex-constant-2015-USD.pdf. On troop deployments, see Tim Kane, "Global U.S. Troop Deployment, 1950–2005," https://www.heritage.org/defense/report/global-us-troop-deployment-1950-2005.

21. George Stephanopoulos, *All Too Human: A Political Education* (Boston: Little, Brown, 1999), 214.

22. James Lindsay, "The New Apathy: How an Uninterested Public Is Reshaping Foreign Policy," *Foreign Affairs* 79, no. 5 (2000): 4.

23. Francis Fukuyama, "The End of History?" *National Interest* 16 (1989): 3–18.

24. Thomas Friedman, *The Lexus and the Olive Tree: Understanding Globalization* (New York: Farrar, Straus, and Giroux, 2000), ix.

25. Michael Mandelbaum, *The Ideas That Conquered the World: Peace, Democracy, and Free Markets in the Twenty-First Century* (New York: PublicAffairs, 2003), 5.

26. G. John Ikenberry, "The Future of the Liberal World Order: Internationalism After America," *Foreign Affairs* 90, no. 3 (2011): 61.

27. On this point, see Walter Russell Mead, "The Return of Geopolitics: The Revenge of the Revisionist Powers," *Foreign Affairs* 93, no. 3 (2014): 69–73; Thomas Wright, *All Measures Short of War: The Contest for the 21st Century and the Future of American Power* (New Haven: Yale University Press, 2017).

28. Bush, "Address Before a Joint Session of the Congress on the Persian Gulf Crisis and the Federal Budget Deficit."

29. Bill Clinton, *My Life* (New York: Knopf, 2004), 956.

30. *The National Security Strategy of the United States of America*, September 2002, https://www.state.gov/documents/organization/63562.pdf.

31. See Robert Zoellick, "Whither China: From Membership to Responsibility?" Remarks to National Committee on U.S.-China Relations, September 21, 2005, https://2001-2009.state.gov/s/d/former/zoellick/rem/53682.htm.

32. Condoleezza Rice, *No Higher Honor: A Memoir of My Years in Washington* (New York: Crown, 2011), 586.

33. National Intelligence Council, *Global Trends 2025: A Transformed World*, vi, https://www.dni.gov/files/documents/Newsroom/Reports%20and%20Pubs/2025_Global_Trends_Final_Report.pdf.

34. For greater detail, see the discussion in chapter 6.

35. SIPRI Database, https://www.sipri.org/sites/default/files/Milex-constant
-2015-USD.pdf; Katherine Blakely, *Analysis of the FY 2017 Defense Budget and
Trends in Defense Spending* (Washington, DC: Center for Strategic and Budgetary Assessments, 2016), iv.

36. World Bank, "Military Expenditure (% of GDP)," http://data.world
bank.org/indicator/MS.MIL.XPND.GD.ZS?locations=US&page=3.

37. Bernard Brodie, *Strategy in the Missile Age* (Santa Monica, CA: RAND
Corporation, 1959), 358.

38. On shares of the federal budget, see Center on Budget and Policy
Priorities, "Policy Basics: Where Do Our Federal Tax Dollars Go?" October
4, 2017, https://www.cbpp.org/research/federal-budget/policy-basics-where
-do-our-federal-tax-dollars-go.

39. See Congressional Budget Office, *The Budget and Economic Outlook: 2017 to 2027*, January 2017, https://www.cbo.gov/sites/default/files/
115th-congress-2017-2018/reports/52370-outlookonecolumn.pdf.

40. Ed Keefe, "Former Pentagon Chiefs to Congress: If You're Serious About
Defense, Don't Pass Current GOP Tax Bill," *Washington Post*, November 15,
2017; Richard Rubin, "Senate Tax Bill Will Add $1.4467 Trillion to Deficit,
CBO Says," *Wall Street Journal*, December 2, 2017.

41. See Frank Newport, "Americans Not Convinced U.S. Needs to Spend
More on Defense," *Gallup News*, February 21, 2018, http://news.gallup.com/
poll/228137/americans-not-convinced-needs-spend-defense.aspx; Aaron
Mehta, "DoD Needs 3–5 Percent Annual Growth Through 2023, Top Officials
Say," *Defense News*, June 13, 2017; Colin Clark, "U.S. 'Will Lose Ability to Project
Power' in 5 Years if Hill Doesn't Act: CJCS," *Breaking Defense*, June 12, 2017. By
2017, the consensus among the DOD civilian and military leadership was that
the United States required 3–5 percent annual growth above inflation over
at least a five-year period to sustain its power-projection capabilities. As of
2018, however, the Trump administration was planning for military spending
to be roughly flat—in real terms—after fiscal year 2019.

42. Connor O'Brien, "Military Hawks Win Big in Budget Deal—For Now,"
Politico, February 9, 2018.

43. Travis Tritten, "Service Chiefs Paint Bleak Picture Ahead of Defense
Budget," *Stars and Stripes*, September 15, 2016.

44. Department of Defense, *Sustaining U.S. Global Leadership: Priorities for 21st Century Defense*, January 2012, http://archive.defense.gov/news/
Defense_Strategic_Guidance.pdf; Department of Defense, *Summary of the
2018 National Defense Strategy of the United States of America*, January 2018,
https://www.defense.gov/Portals/1/Documents/pubs/2018-National-Defense
-Strategy-Summary.pdf.

45. William S. Cohen, *Report of the Quadrennial Defense Review,* May 1997, http://www.bits.de/NRANEU/others/strategy/qdr97.pdf.

46. Gary Clyde Hufbauer and Zhiyao Lu, "The Payoff to America from Globalization: A Fresh Look with a Focus to Costs to Workers," Peterson Institute for International Economics, Policy Brief 17-16, May 2017, esp. 1.

47. Douglas Irwin, *Clashing over Commerce: A History of U.S. Trade Policy* (Chicago: University of Chicago Press, 2017), 688.

48. Pew Research Center, "Public Uncertain, Divided over America's Place in the World," May 5, 2016, http://www.people-press.org/2016/05/05/public -uncertain-divided-over-americas-place-in-the-world/.

49. "Most Applaud End of TPP, Want Changes in NAFTA," *Rasmussen Reports,* January 26, 2017.

50. See Dani Rodrik, "The Great Globalisation Lie," *Prospect,* December 12, 2017; Daron Acemoglu et al., "Import Competition and the Great U.S. Employ-ment Sag of the 2000s," *Journal of Labor Economics* 34, no. S1 (2016): S141–98.

51. Charles Kupchan and Peter Trubowitz, "Dead Center: The Demise of Liberal Internationalism in the United States," *International Security* 32, no. 2 (2007): 7–44; Irwin, *Clashing over Commerce,* 658.

52. Pew Research Center, "Americans Put Low Priority on Promoting Democracy Abroad," December 4, 2013, http://www.pewresearch.org/fact -tank/2013/12/04/americans-put-low-priority-on-promoting-democracy -abroad/.

53. See, for instance, Thom Shanker, "Defense Secretary Warns NATO of 'Dim' Future," *New York Times,* June 10, 2011.

54. Pew Research Center, "Most Say U.S. Should 'Not Get Too Involved' in Ukraine Situation," March 11, 2014, http://www.people-press.org/2014/03/11/ most-say-u-s-should-not-get-too-involved-in-ukraine-situation/.

55. Jacob Heilbrunn, "The Myth of the New Isolationism," *National Inter-est* 128 (2013): 5.

56. Pew Research Center, "Public Sees U.S. Power Declining as Support for Global Engagement Slips," December 3, 2013, http://www.people-press .org/2013/12/03/public-sees-u-s-power-declining-as-support-for-global -engagement-slips/.

57. Pew Research Center, "Key Findings on How Americans View the U.S. Role in the World," May 5, 2016, http://www.pewresearch.org/fact -tank/2016/05/05/key-findings-on-how-americans-view-the-u-s-role-in -the-world/.

58. Chicago Council on Global Affairs, "Chapter 1: U.S. Role in the World," in *2014 Chicago Council Survey: Foreign Policy in the Age of Retrenchment,* http://survey.thechicagocouncil.org/survey/2014/chapter1.html; Gallup News,

"Most Important Problem," http://news.gallup.com/poll/1675/most-important
-problem.aspx.

59. Pew Research Center, "On Eve of Inauguration, Americans Expect
Nation's Deep Political Divisions to Persist," January 19, 2017, http://www
.people-press.org/2017/01/19/on-eve-of-inauguration-americans-expect
-nations-deep-political-divisions-to-persist/.

60. Dina Smeltz, Ivo Daalder, Karl Friedhoff, and Craig Kafura, *America
in the Age of Uncertainty* (Chicago: Chicago Council on Global Affairs, 2016).

61. Oona Hathaway and Scott Shapiro, *The Internationalists: How a Radical
Plan to Outlaw War Remade the World* (New York: Simon & Schuster, 2017);
Steven Pinker, *Better Angels of Our Nature: Why Violence Has Declined* (New
York: Viking, 2011).

62. On offshore balancing, see Christopher Layne, "Offshore Balancing
Revisited," *Washington Quarterly* 25, no. 2 (2002): 233–248. For a critique, see
Hal Brands, *American Grand Strategy in the Age of Trump* (Washington, DC:
Brookings Institution Press, 2018), chapter 2.

63. Peter Baker and Michael Shear, "Obama Trumpets Killing of Bin Laden,
and Critics Pounce," *New York Times,* April 27, 2012.

64. Council on Foreign Relations, "A Conversation with U.S. Secretary
of State Hillary Rodham Clinton," July 15, 2009, https://www.cfr.org/event/
conversation-us-secretary-state-hillary-rodham-clinton-1.

65. *National Security Strategy,* May 2010, http://nssarchive.us/NSSR/2010
.pdf, 3; Wright, *All Measures Short of War.*

66. Jillian Rayfield, "Obama: The '80s Called, They Want Their Foreign
Policy Back," *Salon.com,* October 22, 2012, https://www.salon.com/2012/10/23/
obama_the_80s_called_they_want_their_foreign_policy_back/.

67. David Larter, "White House Tells the Pentagon to Quit Talking About
'Competition' with China," *Navy Times,* September 26, 2016; Jeffrey Goldberg,
"The Obama Doctrine," *The Atlantic,* April 2016, https://www.theatlantic.com/
magazine/archive/2016/04/the-obama-doctrine/471525/.

68. Jaime Fuller, "Kerry Says 'Russia Is Going to Lose' if Putin's Troops
Continue to Advance in Ukraine," *Washington Post,* March 2, 2014.

69. For instance, Leon Panetta, "How the White House Misplayed Iraqi
Troop Talks," *Time,* October 1, 2014; Dexter Filkins, "What We Left Behind,"
New Yorker, April 28, 2014, http://www.newyorker.com/magazine/2014/04/28/
what-we-left-behind.

70. See Tim Hains, "Gen. Petraeus: Syria Has Become a 'Geopolitical Chernobyl' Spewing Instability Worldwide," *Real Clear Politics,* September 22, 2015.

71. Ely Ratner, "Course Correction: How to Stop China's Maritime Advance," *Foreign Affairs* 96, no. 4 (2017): 66–67.

72. See, for instance, Goldberg, "The Obama Doctrine"; "Obama's Address on the War in Afghanistan," *New York Times,* December 1, 2009.

73. Quoted in Mike Allen, *Politico Playbook,* June 1, 2014, https://www.politico.com/tipsheets/playbook/2014/06/brunch-edition-forget-leading-from-behind-and-singles-doubles-west-wing-has-its-own-obama-doctrine-shorthand-hagel-in-afghanistan-lehane-fabiani-update-212543.

74. "Open Letter on Donald Trump from GOP National Security Leaders," *War on the Rocks,* March 2, 2016; also Thomas Wright, "Trump's 19th Century Foreign Policy," *Politico,* January 20, 2016; Hal Brands and Colin Kahl, "Trump's Grand Strategic Train-Wreck," *Foreign Policy,* January 31, 2017.

75. Charles Edel, "Trump and the American Presidency: The Past, Present, and Future of America's Highest Office," February 27, 2018. https://www.ussc.edu.au/analysis/us-presidency-past-present-future-trump-impact.

76. *National Security Strategy of the United States of America,* December 2017, https://www.whitehouse.gov/wp-content/uploads/2017/12/NSS-Final-12-18-2017-0905.pdf; Department of Defense, *Summary of the National Defense Strategy of the United States of America*; Idrees Ali, "Trump to Ask for $716 Billion in Defense Spending in 2019 Budget: U.S. Officials," *Reuters,* January 26, 2018.

77. "The Inaugural Address," January 20, 2017, https://www.whitehouse.gov/briefings-statements/the-inaugural-address/; also Eliot Cohen, "How Trump Is Ending the American Era," *The Atlantic,* October 2017, https://www.theatlantic.com/magazine/archive/2017/10/is-trump-ending-the-american-era/537888/; G. John Ikenberry, "The Plot Against American Foreign Policy: Can the Liberal Order Survive?" *Foreign Affairs* 96, no. 3 (2017): 2–8; Brands, *American Grand Strategy in the Age of Trump,* chapter 6.

6
The Darkening Horizon

1. Henry Adams, *The Education of Henry Adams* (New York: Modern Library, 1931), 381.

2. Portions of this chapter are drawn from Hal Brands and Charles Edel, "The Disharmony of the Spheres," *Commentary,* January 2018, 20–27; and the text originally written by Brands in two pieces: Hal Brands and Eric Edelman, *Why Is the World So Unsettled? The End of the Post–Cold War Era and the Crisis of Global Order* (Washington, DC: Center for Strategic and Budgetary Assessments, 2017); Hal Brands and Eric Edelman, "The Upheaval," *National Interest* 150 (2017): 30–40.

3. Brian Murphy, "DNI Clapper Provides Series of Threat Assessments on Capitol Hill," February 29, 2016, https://www.dni.gov/index.php/newsroom/item/1334-dni-clapper-provides-series-of-threat-assessments-on-capitol-hill.

4. Barack Obama, "Now Is the Greatest Time to Be Alive," *Wired*, October 12, 2016.

5. Winston Churchill, *The Gathering Storm* (New York: Houghton Mifflin, 1948).

6. Statistics from Hal Brands, *Dealing with Allies in Decline: Alliance Management and U.S. Strategy in an Era of Global Power Shifts* (Washington, DC: Center for Strategic and Budgetary Assessments, 2017), 5–8.

7. World Bank, "GDP per Capita, PPP (Current International $)," http://data.worldbank.org/indicator/NY.GDP.PCAP.PP.CD?order=wbapi_data_value_2013+wbapi_data_value+wbapi_data_valuelast&sort=desc; SIPRI Military Expenditures Database; Stephen Brooks and William Wohlforth, "The Once and Future Superpower: Why China Won't Overtake the United States," *Foreign Affairs* 95, no. 3 (2016): 91–92.

8. World Bank, "GDP (constant 2010 US$)," available at https://data.worldbank.org/indicator/NY.GDP.MKTP.KD?locations=RU-CN.

9. Justin Huggler, "German Army Used Broomsticks Instead of Guns During Training," *Telegraph*, February 18, 2015; Nicholas M. Gallagher, "When Britain Really Ruled the Waves," *The American Interest*, November 14, 2014.

10. Brands, *Dealing with Allies in Decline*.

11. International Institute for Strategic Studies, *The Military Balance 2015*, 159–167; Catrin Einhorn, Hannah Fairfield, and Tim Wallace, "Russia Rearms for a New Era," *New York Times*, December 24, 2015.

12. SIPRI Military Expenditure Database; U.S. Department of Agriculture, Economic Research Service, "GDP Shares by Country and Region Historical," https://www.ers.usda.gov/data-products/international-macroeconomic-data-set.aspx; Brands, *Dealing with Allies in Decline*, 22; Evan Montgomery, "Contested Primacy in the Western Pacific: China's Rise and the Future of U.S. Power Projection," *International Security* 38, no. 4 (2014): 115–149.

13. Peter Hayes Gries, "China Eyes the Hegemon," *Orbis*, Summer 2005, 406.

14. Jeffrey Bader, *Obama and China's Rise: An Insider's Account of America's Asia Strategy* (Washington, DC: Brookings Institution Press, 2012), 80.

15. *National Security Strategy of the United States of America*, 2010, 1, http://nssarchive.us/NSSR/2010.pdf.

16. On the general phenomenon, see A. Wess Mitchell and Jakub Grygiel, *The Unquiet Frontier: Rising Rivals, Vulnerable Allies, and the Crisis of American Power* (Princeton, NJ: Princeton University Press, 2016).

17. Aaron Friedberg, *A Contest for Supremacy: China, America, and the Struggle for Mastery in Asia* (New York: Norton, 2011), 2.

18. Manu Pubby, "China Proposed Division of Pacific, Indian Ocean Regions, We Declined: U.S. Admiral," *Indian Express*, May 15, 2009.

19. See John Pomfret, "U.S. Takes a Tougher Tone with China," *Washington Post*, July 30, 2010.

20. Good accounts of Chinese behavior include Office of the Secretary of Defense (OSD), *Military and Security Developments Involving the People's Republic of China 2016, Annual Report to Congress* (Washington, DC: Department of Defense, 2016); Howard French, *Everything Under the Heavens: How the Past Helps Shape China's Push for Global Power* (New York: Knopf, 2017); Anne-Marie Brady, "Magic Weapons: China's Political Influence Activities Under Xi Jinping," https://www.wilsoncenter.org/sites/default/files/for_website_magicweaponsanne-mariesbradyseptember2017.pdf.

21. Ben Blanchard, "Duterte Aligns Philippines with China, Says U.S. Has Lost," *Reuters*, October 20, 2016.

22. Eric Heginbotham et al., *The U.S.–China Military Scorecard: Forces, Geography, and the Evolving Balance of Power, 1996–2017* (Santa Monica, CA: RAND Corporation, 2015), 342, xxxi.

23. See Fyodor Lukyanov, "The Lost Twenty-Five Years," *Global Brief,* February 19, 2016.

24. "Boris Johnson Claims Russia Was Behind Plot to Assassinate Prime Minister of Montenegro as He Warns of Putin's 'Dirty Tricks,' " *The Telegraph*, March 12, 2017. See also Heather Conley et al., *The Kremlin Playbook: Understanding Russian Influence in Central and Eastern Europe* (Washington, DC: Center for Strategic and International Studies, 2016).

25. For a discussion, see Molly McKew, "The Gerasimov Doctrine," *Politico,* September 5, 2017.

26. Anna Borshchevskaya and Jeremy Vaughan, "How the Russian Military Reestablished Itself in the Middle East," Policy Watch 2709, Washington Institute for Near East Policy, October 17, 2016.

27. Lizzie Dearden, "Russia's Foreign Minister Calls for 'Post-West World Order' in Speech to Global Leaders," *Independent,* February 18, 2017.

28. David A. Shlapak and Michael W. Johnson, "Outnumbered, Outranged, and Outgunned: How Russia Defeats NATO," *War on the Rocks*, April 21, 2016.

29. Douglas Ernst, "Putin Says He Could Have Troops Inside Poland 'In Two Days': Report," *Washington Times,* September 18, 2014.

30. Afshon Ostovar, *Vanguard of the Imam: Religion, Politics, and Iran's Revolutionary Guard* (New York: Oxford University Press, 2016), 205.

31. In May 2018, President Trump announced that the United States was effectively withdrawing from the Iran nuclear deal, casting the fate of that agreement into uncertainty and raising the prospect that Tehran might resume uranium enrichment or other steps toward obtaining nuclear weapons.

32. Julian Borger and Patrick Wintour, "U.S. Gives Evidence Iran Supplied Missiles that Yemen Rebels Fired at Saudi Arabia," *The Guardian,* December 14, 2017.

33. Ben Hubbard, Isabel Kershner, and Anne Barnard, "Iran, Deeply Embedded in Syria, Expands 'Axis of Resistance,'" *New York Times,* February 19, 2018.

34. Bob Savic, "Behind China and Russia's Special Relationship," *The Diplomat,* December 7, 2016; Robin Wright, "Russia and Iran Deepen Ties to Challenge Trump and the United States," *New Yorker,* March 2, 2018.

35. "Navy Official: China Training for 'Short Sharp War' with Japan," *USNI News,* February 18, 2014; Max Fisher, "How World War III Became Possible: A Nuclear Conflict with Russia Is Likelier Than You Think," *Vox,* June 29, 2015.

36. Ellen Nakashima, Karen DeYoung, and Liz Sly, "Putin Ally Said to Be in Touch with Kremlin, Assad Before His Mercenaries Attacked U.S. Troops," *Washington Post,* February 22, 2018.

37. Scott Wilson, "Obama Dismisses Russia as 'Regional Power' Acting Out of Weakness," *Washington Post,* March 25, 2014.

38. See "Xi Jinping: 'Time for China to Take Centre Stage,'" *BBC News,* October 18, 2017; Evan Osnos, "Making China Great Again," *New Yorker,* January 8, 2018.

39. See Robert Kagan, "The Twilight of the Liberal World Order," January 24, 2017, https://www.brookings.edu/research/the-twilight-of-the-liberal-world-order/.

40. *A National Security Strategy of Engagement and Enlargement* (Washington, DC: The White House, 1995), iii.

41. Larry Diamond, *Developing Democracy: Toward Consolidation* (Baltimore, MD: Johns Hopkins University Press, 1999), 25; Freedom House, *Freedom in the World 2013: Democratic Breakthroughs in the Balance,* https://freedomhouse.org/sites/default/files/FIW%202013%20Booklet.pdf.

42. Freedom House, *Freedom in the World 2018: Democracy in Crisis,* https://freedomhouse.org/report/freedom-world/freedom-world-2018.

43. On polling data, see Roberto Stefan Foa and Yascha Mounk, "The Signs of Deconsolidation," *Journal of Democracy* 28, no. 1 (2017): 5–16.

44. William Dobson, *The Dictator's Learning Curve: Inside the Global Battle for Democracy* (New York: Doubleday, 2012); Erica Frantz and Andrea Kendall-Taylor, "The Evolution of Autocracy: Why Authoritarianism Is Becoming More Formidable," *Survival* 59, no. 5 (2017): 57–68.

45. Full text of Viktor Orbán's speech at Băile Tușnad (Tusnádfürdő) of July 26, 2014, https://budapestbeacon.com/full-text-of-viktor-orbans-speech-at-baile-tusnad-tusnadfurdo-of-26-july-2014/.

46. Larry Diamond, "The Liberal Democratic Order in Crisis," *The American Interest,* February 16, 2018.

47. Larry Diamond, Marc Plattner, and Christopher Walker, eds., *Authoritarianism Goes Global: The Challenge to Democracy* (Baltimore: Johns Hopkins University Press, 2016), 4. See also the essays by Alexander Cooley, "Countering Democratic Norms," and Andrew Nathan, "China's Challenge," in the foregoing volume; Michael Clarke and Raffaello Pantucci, "China Is Supporting Syria's Regime. What Changed?" *National Interest,* September 17, 2016.

48. John Cipher and Steve Hall, "Oh, Wait. Maybe It Was Collusion," *New York Times,* August 2, 2017.

49. See Brady, "Magic Weapons"; Thorston Benner, Jan Gaspers, Mareike Ohlberg, Lucrezia Poggetti, and Kristin Shi-Kupfer, "Authoritarian Advance: Responding to China's Growing Political Influence in Europe," Mercator Institute for China Studies, February 2018.

50. "Sharp Power: The New Shape of Chinese Power," *The Economist,* December 16, 2017; Joseph Nye, "How Sharp Power Threatens Soft Power," *Foreign Affairs,* January 24, 2018.

51. Karl Popper, *The Open Society and Its Enemies* (Princeton, NJ: Princeton University Press, 2013), 127.

52. Robert Kagan, *The Return of History and the End of Dreams* (New York: Alfred A. Knopf, 2008); Aaron L. Friedberg, "The Authoritarian Challenge: China, Russia and the Threat to the Liberal International Order," Sasakawa Peace Foundation, August 2017, https://www.spf.org/jpus-j/img/investigation/The_Authoritarian_Challenge.pdf.

53. James Woolsey, "Hearing before the Select Committee on Intelligence of the United States Senate," February 2–3, 1993, https://www.intelligence.senate.gov/sites/default/files/hearings/103296.pdf.

54. Hedley Bull, *The Anarchical Society: A Study of Order in World Politics* (New York: Columbia University Press, 1977).

55. See William McCants, *ISIS Apocalypse: The History, Strategy, and Doomsday Vision of the Islamic State* (New York: Picador, 2015); James Fromson and Steven Simon, "ISIS: The Dubious Paradise of Apocalypse Now," *Survival* 57, no. 3 (2015).

56. On this analogy, see Brendan Simms, Michael Axworthy, and Patrick Milton, "Ending the New Thirty Years War," *New Statesman,* January 26, 2016.

57. Richard Haass, *A World in Disarray: American Foreign Policy and the Crisis of the Old Order* (New York: Penguin, 2016), 150.

58. Strobe Talbott, *The Russia Hand: A Memoir of Presidential Diplomacy* (New York: Random House, 2002), chapters 7–8.

59. "Read Putin's U.N. General Assembly Speech," *Washington Post,* September 28, 2015.

60. Thomas Rid, "How Russia Pulled Off the Biggest Election Hack in U.S. History," *Esquire,* October 20, 2016; Ellen Nakashima, "Chinese Breach Data of 4 Million Federal Workers," *Washington Post,* June 4, 2015.

61. James Kirchick, *The End of Europe: Dictators, Demagogues, and the Coming Dark Age* (New Haven: Yale University Press, 2017); Craig Winneker, "For Europe's NATO Allies, Attack on One Isn't Attack on All," *Politico Europe,* June 10, 2015; Shi Zhiqin and Lai Suetyi, "Xi's Visit to Kick Off a Golden Age of China-UK Relations," *The Diplomat,* October 15, 2015.

62. Jeffrey Goldberg, "The Obama Doctrine," *The Atlantic,* April 2016, https://www.theatlantic.com/magazine/archive/2016/04/the-obama-doctrine/471525/.

63. Richard Wike, Bruce Stokes, Jacob Poushter, and Janell Fetterolf, "U.S. Image Suffers as Publics Around World Question Trump's Leadership," Pew Research Center, June 26, 2017, http://www. pewglobal.org/2017/06/26/u-s-image-suffers-as-publics-around-world-question-trumps-leadership/.

64. Susan Glasser, "Trump National Security Team Blindsided by NATO Speech," *Politico,* June 5, 2017; Krishnadev Calamur, "Merkel Urges 'Europe to Take Our Fate into Our Own Hands,'" *The Atlantic,* May 30, 2017.

65. Bill Hayton, "The Week Donald Trump Lost the South China Sea," *Foreign Policy,* July 31, 2017; James Bowen, "Trump–Turnbull Meeting Comes Amid Increasing Debate over Australia's U.S. Ties," *The Diplomat,* May 5, 2017; Hans Mouritzen, "Small States and Finlandisation in the Age of Trump," *Survival* 59, no. 2 (2017): 67–84.

66. Adam Behsudi, "Trump's Trade Pullout Roils Rural America," *Politico,* August 7, 2017; William Horobin, "France Looks to Deepen Trade Ties with Russia and China," *Wall Street Journal,* December 29, 2017.

67. Osnos, "Making China Great Again."

68. Louis Halle, *Civilization and Foreign Policy: An Inquiry for Americans* (New York: Harper and Brothers, 1955), 262.

7
Rediscovering Tragedy

1. Robert C. Pirro, *Hannah Arendt and the Politics of Tragedy* (DeKalb: Northern Illinois University Press, 2001), 41–42.

2. Albin Lesky, *Greek Tragedy,* trans. H. A. Frankfort (London: Ernest Benn, 1965), 9.

3. Thucydides, *Landmark Thucydides*, III.81.

4. Robert Gilpin, *War and Change in World Politics* (New York: Cambridge University Press, 1983), 194.

5. Daniel Twining, "Abandoning the Liberal International Order for a Spheres-of-Influence World Is a Trap for America and Its Allies," German Marshall Fund of the United States, June 2, 2017; Robert Kagan, "Backing into World War III," *Foreign Policy,* February 6, 2017.

6. Nietzsche quoted in Edith Hamilton, *The Greek Way* (New York: Norton, 1942), 239. This quotation is often used, but its exact provenance is difficult to determine. It appears to be Hamilton's somewhat stylized translation or paraphrase of key passages from Nietzsche, *Birth of Tragedy.*

7. "GDP Shares by Country and Region Historical," International Macroeconomic Data Set, Economic Research Service, U.S. Department of Agriculture, https://www.ers.usda.gov/data-products/international -macroeconomic-data-set.aspx; SIPRI Fact Sheet, "Trends in World Military Expenditure, 2016," April 2017, https://www.sipri.org/sites/default/files/ Trends-world-military-expenditure-2016.pdf; Hal Brands, *Dealing with Allies in Decline: Alliance Management and U.S. Strategy in an Era of Global Power Shifts* (Washington, DC: Center for Strategic and Budgetary Assessments, 2017).

8. Adam Taylor, "The U.S. Is Bound by Treaties to Defend a Quarter of Humanity," *Washington Post,* May 30, 2015.

9. John Lewis Gaddis, *The Long Peace: Inquiries into the History of the Cold War* (New York: Oxford University Press, 1986), 57.

10. John F. Kennedy, "Inaugural Address," January 20, 1961, APP.

11. One of the common objections to calls for the United States to spend more on defense is the idea that this is unaffordable in light of spiraling entitlement commitments, and that reducing entitlement spending will simply fuel the domestic economic insecurity that is alienating Americans from the internationalist tradition. Yet here as elsewhere, the problem is perhaps less intractable, at least from an economic perspective, than sometimes thought. As countless experts have noted, there are plausible steps that would rein in the costs of programs such as Social Security without depriving the economically insecure of badly needed benefits: means-testing, for instance, or raising the retirement age to reflect the fact that the proportion of Americans working in physically labor-intensive jobs has dropped dramatically since the 1930s or even the 1980s. The available revenues could also be increased significantly with tax increases. Put another way, the fact that the richest country in the world seems to confront such difficulty in spending perhaps 4 percent of GDP on defense while also providing a bare level of economic

security for the insecure is more a testament to political constraints than economic ones.

12. John Lewis Gaddis, *George F. Kennan: An American Life* (New York: Penguin, 2011), 264.

13. Norman Kempster, "Baker Says Iraqi Threat Calls for Defense Alliance," *Los Angeles Times*, September 5, 1990.

14. This is one of many Lenin quotes that are impossible to pin down. The closest published formulation is in Richard Pipes, ed., *The Unknown Lenin: From the Secret Archive* (New Haven: Yale University Press, 1996), 100.

15. Thomas Schelling, *Arms and Influence* (New Haven: Yale University Press, 1966), 124.

16. See Charles Edel, "Limiting Chinese Aggression: A Strategy of Counter-Pressure," *The American Interest*, February 9, 2018. https://www. the-american-interest.com/2018/02/09/limiting-chinese-aggression-strategy -counter-pressure/.

17. Vincent Sheean, *Between the Thunder and the Sea* (New York: Random House, 1943), 56.

18. Robert Vansittart, *The Mist Procession: The Autobiography of Lord Vansittart* (London: Hutchinson, 1958), 28.

19. Stephen Sestanovich, *Maximalist: America in the World from Truman to Obama* (New York: Knopf, 2014), 9.

20. Reinhold Niebuhr, *The Irony of American History* (New York: Charles Scribner and Sons, 1952), 130.

21. Robert Jervis, *Perception and Misperception in International Politics* (Princeton, NJ: Princeton University Press, 2017), 239.

22. The power/willpower point is also made in Robert Lieber, *Power and Willpower in the American Future: Why the United States Is Not Destined to Decline* (New York: Cambridge University Press, 2012).

23. Henry A. Kissinger, *A World Restored: Metternich, Castlereagh, and the Problems of Peace, 1812–1822* (Boston: Houghton Mifflin, 1973), 6.

Index

Abdullah II, king of Jordan, 142
Abyssinia, 160
Acheson, Dean, 68, 72, 75, 76, 78, 81, 83, 84
Adams, Henry, 118
Aeschylus, 1–2, 10, 11–14, 15, 19, 27
Afghanistan, 102, 104, 107, 110, 121
Agamemnon (Aeschylus), 1–2, 17
Albright, Madeleine, 94
Alcestis (Euripides), 15
Alexander I, emperor of Russia, 48
al-Qaeda, 94, 139
Anarchical Society, The (Bull), 137
Angell, Norman, 35, 99, 147
Antigone (Sophocles), 9
Arabian Peninsula, 138
Arab Spring, 127
Arctic, 130
Aristophanes, 9–10
Aristotle, 3, 11
Armenian genocide, 37
Asian Infrastructure Investment Bank (AIIB), 124, 131
Assad, Bashar al-, 108, 126, 128, 134, 140
Association of Southeast Asian Nations (ASEAN), 123

Athens: cultural and economic apogee of, 27; decline of, 18, 20; democracy in, 7, 16, 17; as a sea power, 26; Sparta vs., 7, 19, 25–28, 84; theater in, 2–3, 7–9; wartime strains in, 15
Atlantic Charter (1941), 79
atomic weapons. *See* nuclear weapons
Australia, 124
Austria, 48, 50, 56, 76
Austro-Hungarian Empire, 36, 56
authoritarianism, 6, 59, 118, 138, 149, 161; in China, 133–135, 136, 150, 153

Bacchae (Euripides), 9
Baker, James, 92, 158
balance of power, 6, 24, 25; during Cold War, 74, 75, 85; idealism vs., 53; importance of, 118–119; Napoleonic Wars and, 33, 49; Peace of Westphalia and, 43, 45, 46–47; U.S. fatigue and, 121–122; World War I and, 36, 57
Baldwin, Stanley, 40, 61
Balkans, 36, 95, 138

Battle of Leipzig (1813), 34
Battle of Marathon (490 BC), 13
Battle of Salamis (480 BC), 13
Bell, David, 34
Belt and Road Initiative (BRI), 124,
    131
Berlin, 82
Berlin, Isaiah, 83
Berlin Wall, 93
Bin Laden, Osama, 110
Birth of Tragedy, The (Nietzsche), 10
Bismarck, Otto von, 51, 164
Bohemia, 30
Bohlen, Charles, 154
Bolshevik Revolution, 56
Bosnia, 140
Bourbon, House of, 33
Bretton Woods system, 71–72
Brodie, Bernard, 103
Brooks, Stephen, 120
Buchanan, Pat, 97–98
Budget Control Act (BCA), 104
Bull, Hedley, 137
Bush, George H. W., 23, 92–93, 97,
    100
Bush, George W., 23, 100–101, 102,
    107, 109, 113, 142

Cameron, David, 141
Castlereagh, Robert Stewart,
    Viscount, 47–51
catharsis, 3, 11
Catholics, 30, 44, 46
Cecil, Lord Robert, 39
Central Asia, 126, 131
Central Europe, 46, 59, 68
Chamberlain, Neville, 39, 60, 62
chemical weapons, 138–139, 159
China, 68, 95, 100, 101, 125;
    authoritarianism in, 133–135, 136,

150, 153; economic rise of, 107,
    119–120, 122; global ambitions of,
    112, 119, 123–124, 130–131, 141–142,
    144, 159; military buildup by, 103,
    121, 124, 127, 130, 142; Obama's
    policies toward, 111, 112; Russian
    collaboration with, 128
Churchill, Winston, 38, 160
CIA (Central Intelligence Agency),
    84
Civil War, U.S., 41
Clapper, James, 118
Clausewitz, Carl von, 34
Clemenceau, Georges, 54, 57
climate change, 100, 111
Clinton, Bill, 94, 96, 97, 98, 100, 132,
    140
Clinton, Hillary, 111
Cold War, 22, 73–81, 87, 90–94, 97,
    107, 114, 154
communism, 22, 56
complacency, 11, 57, 88, 151
Concert of Europe, 5, 47–52, 53, 56,
    62, 86, 165
Congo, 85
containment, 82, 88
Corcyra, 28
Craig, Gordon, 50
Crimea, 111–112, 130
Crimean War (1853–1856), 51
cuius regio, euius religio, 44
cyberwarfare, 125, 134, 139, 140,
    141
Czechoslovakia, 56

Darius I, king of Persia, 13, 14
defense spending. *See* military
    spending
deficits, 72, 102, 104
de Gaulle, Charles, 82

democracy, 33; Athenian, 7, 16, 17; challenges to, 6, 132–136; post–World War II growth of, 65, 86, 88, 99; U.S. promotion of, 78–79, 92, 94, 95–96, 108
Denmark, 30
Diamond, Larry, 133
Dionysus, 8, 10
diplomacy, 23, 45, 49–50, 60
disarmament, 53, 58, 111
disinformation, 126, 134, 141
Dominican Republic–Central America Free Trade Agreement, 106–107
Dulles, John Foster, 77
Duterte, Rodrigo, 124–125, 142

East China Sea, 124
Education of Henry Adams, The, 117
Egypt, 80, 127
Einstein, Albert, 64–65
Eisenhower, Dwight, 80, 82, 83–84
Emerson, Ralph Waldo, 5
empire, 22–23, 51
England, 29, 46
Enlightenment, 32, 35, 97
entitlements, 104, 190n11
Ethiopia, 76
ethnic conflict, 137, 139–140
Eumenides, The (Aeschylus), 17, 18
Euripides, 9–10, 12, 15, 16–17, 27
European Coal and Steel Community (ECSC), 77
European Community (EC), 77
European Union (EU), 77, 87, 125–126, 141

fake news, 126, 134
fascism, 22, 38, 59

Ferdinand II, Holy Roman Emperor, 43, 44
financial crisis of 2007–2008, 102, 120, 121, 139
Fish, Hamilton, 82
Foch, Ferdinand, 56
foreign aid, 71, 98
Fourteen Points, 53
France, 38; during Cold War, 82; during Hitler's rise, 59, 62; during Napoleonic Wars, 33–34; Quadruple Alliance vs., 48–49; in Thirty Years' War, 30, 45–46; U.S. viewed by, 94; war against Egypt, 80; after World War I, 54, 56
Franz Ferdinand, archduke of Austria, 36
Freedman, Lawrence, 178n67
Freedom House, 132
freedom of the seas, 53, 92, 129, 149, 159
French Revolution, 32–33, 35, 47
Friedberg, Aaron, 122–123
Friedman, Thomas, 99
Frogs (Aristophanes), 9–10
Fukuyama, Francis, 23, 99
Fulda Gap, 74
Fussell, Paul, 40

General Agreement on Tariffs and Trade (GATT), 70
George, Alexander, 50
Georgia, 125, 134
Gerasimov, Valery, 126
Germany, 51; global ambitions of, 36; military spending by, 120–121; reunification of, 93; U.S. allied with, 70, 75, 82, 87, 95; Versailles Treaty and, 38, 54–57

Gingrich, Newt, 98
globalization: governance gap
    linked to, 139; growth of, 86;
    peace and stability linked to, 23,
    24, 35, 99; skepticism toward,
    106, 107, 114, 115; U.S. leadership
    linked to, 92, 94, 96. *See also*
    protectionism
Goebbels, Joseph, 59
gold standard, 71
Great Britain, 38; exit from EU by,
    141; invasion of Egypt by, 80;
    military spending by, 59, 120;
    Napoleonic Wars and, 48–49
Great Depression, 38, 58, 60, 66, 67,
    68, 71, 83
Greece: ancient (*see* Athens);
    during Cold War, 76, 79
Greek Way, The (Hamilton), 2
Grew, Joseph, 65
Grotius, Hugo, 45, 55

Haiti, 96
Halberstam, David, 97
Halifax, Edward Frederick Lindley
    Wood, Earl of, 62
Halle, Louis, 144
Hamilton, Edith, 2, 7–8
Heilbrunn, Jacob, 108
Helms, Jesse, 98
Hemingway, Ernest, 61
Heracleidae (Euripides), 15, 16
Herodotus, 13
Hezbollah, 128, 138
Hippocrates, 27
History of the Peloponnesian War
    (Thucydides), 18–21
Hitler, Adolf, 39, 59, 62, 78
Hobbes, Thomas, 24, 42
Hobsbawm, Eric, 65, 66

Hoffman, Paul, 82
Holmes, Oliver Wendell, Jr., 41
Holy Roman Empire, 30, 31, 44, 47
Holy See, 44
Hong Kong, 134
Horn of Africa, 130, 139
Howard, Michael, 29
hubris, 11, 14, 19, 161, 162, 165
Hufbauer, Gary Clyde, 106
human rights, 5, 32, 65, 78, 86, 88,
    92, 139, 156
Hungary, 132, 133
Huntington, Samuel, 94
Hussein, Saddam, 92, 93, 94, 98

Ikenberry, G. John, 42, 100
immigration, 141
India, 124
Indian Ocean, 130
Indonesia, 85
international institutions, 68, 77
international law, 53, 87, 110
International Monetary Fund
    (IMF), 70, 77
Iphigenia at Aulis (Euripides), 15–16
Iran: authoritarianism in, 133;
    nuclear program of, 110, 128, 143;
    regional ambitions of, 127–129,
    134, 138; Russian cooperation
    with, 126; Soviet pressure on, 79;
    U.S. containment of, 95
Iraq, 95; Islamic State in, 137–138;
    U.S. invasion of, 94, 102, 104, 107,
    112, 121, 127, 161
Islamic State, 108, 137–138, 139
Israel, 128
Italy, 38, 85

Japan, 37, 38; Chinese pressure
    on, 124, 125, 141–142; economic

power of, 119; Manchuria
invaded by, 39; U.S. allied with,
70, 71, 75, 82, 87, 95, 119, 120
Johnson, Lyndon, 85
Johnson, Samuel, 12

Kagan, Donald, 4, 63
Kant, Immanuel, 33
Kellogg-Briand Pact (1928), 39, 58
Kennan, George, 58, 82, 84–85, 156
Kennedy, Jacqueline, 2
Kennedy, John F., 2, 72, 81, 83,
154–155
Kennedy, Robert F., 1–2
Kerry, John, 111, 127
Keynes, John Maynard, 80
Keynesianism, 71
Khamenei, Ali, 129
Kim Il Sung, 76
King, Martin Luther, Jr., 1
Kirkpatrick, Jeane, 97
Kissinger, Henry, 51, 83, 86, 102,
165
Korean Peninsula, 74, 128, 159
Kosovo, 119
Kuwait, 93, 160

Law of War and Peace, The
(Grotius), 45
League of Nations, 39, 55, 56, 57, 77,
78, 108
Lebanon, 127
Leffler, Melvyn, 72
Lenin, Vladimir, 159
Lewinsky, Monica, 96
Libation Bearers, The (Aeschylus),
17
Libya, 110, 126, 138
Lippmann, Walter, 60, 84
Lloyd George, David, 38, 61

"Long Telegram" (Kennan),
84–85
Louis XIV, king of France, 46
Lu, Zhiyao, 106
Luce, Henry, 67

Macau, 134
Magdeburg, 31
Manchuria, 39, 59, 76, 160
Mao Zedong, 133
Marshall, George, 3, 5, 69, 73
Marshall Plan, 70, 71, 74, 78, 82, 87
McCloy, John, 81
Mearsheimer, John, 24, 95, 96
Melian Dialogue, 28, 123
mercantilism, 70
Merkel, Angela, 143
Metternich, Klemens von, 47,
49–50
military spending: by Britain, 59,
120; by China, 103, 121, 124, 127,
130, 142; by Germany, 120–121; by
post–Cold War U.S., 97–98, 102,
103–105, 112, 114, 119, 120–121, 152;
by post–World War II U.S., 67,
74–75
Milley, Mark, 105
Milošević, Slobodan, 98
Montenegro, 126, 134
Montesquieu, Charles-Louis de
Secondat, baron de, 32
Morgenthau, Hans, 88–89
Mussolini, Benito, 160
Mutual Security Program, 74
Myanmar, 132

Napoleon Bonaparte, 33, 35,
48, 50
Nasser, Gamal Abdel, 80
nation-states, 23, 42, 44–45

NATO (North Atlantic Treaty
Organization), 87; enlargement
of, 93, 100, 110, 119; European
origins of, 80; frictions within,
108, 141, 157; Russia vs., 119,
125–126, 127; U.S. preeminence
in, 77, 78
Neutrality Acts, 62
Nicholas II, emperor of Russia,
35–36
Niebuhr, Reinhold, 90, 162
Nietzsche, Friedrich, 10, 12, 151
9/11 attacks, 94, 100, 101–102
1984 (Orwell), 88
Nitze, Paul, 75
Nixon, Richard, 83
non-entanglement, 57, 69
non-state actors, 139
North American Free Trade
Agreement (NAFTA), 106–107
North Korea, 76, 95, 137, 149, 162
NSC-*68*, 75
nuclear weapons: American, 40, 67,
74; as deterrent, 87; Iranian
development of, 110, 128, 143;
nonproliferation of, 92, 95, 111;
North Korean, 137, 162; Russian
and Soviet, 83, 129. *See also*
disarmament

Obama, Barack, 109, 118, 122, 130,
144; defense spending cuts and,
104, 105, 112; Syria policy of, 108;
worldview of, 110–113, 142
Oedipus Rex (Sophocles), 9, 11
On Rhetoric (Aristotle), 11
*On the Origins of War and the
Preservation of Peace* (Kagan), 63
Open Society and Its Enemies, The
(Popper), 135

Orban, Viktor, 133
order building: costs of, 109, 164;
war as impetus to, 41–42; after
World War I, 53–54; after World
War II, 66, 69–70, 77–83, 86,
90–91, 164
Oresteia (Aeschylus), 9, 17
Orwell, George, 88
Osnos, Evan, 144
Ottoman Empire, 36
Oxenstierna, Axel, Count, 44
Oxford Union, 61

Patterson, Robert, 68
Peace of Westphalia (1648), 5, 32,
42–47, 50, 53, 56, 62, 146
Peloponnesian War, 3, 7, 16, 18–21,
25–28, 30
Pericles, 19–20
"Perpetual Peace" (Kant), 33
Persian Gulf Crisis and War, 93,
158, 160
Persians, The (Aeschylus), 12–13
Persian Wars, 13
Philippines, 124–125, 132, 134, 142,
143
Phoenician Women, The
(Euripides), 15
Pinker, Steven, 22
Pitt, William, the Younger, 33, 147
plague, 20
Plato, 41
Poland, 56, 96, 132
Popper, Karl, 135
Portugal, 30, 35
Prometheus Bound (Aeschylus), 9
protectionism, 107; European
integration and threat of, 77;
during Great Depression, 58–59,
60, 66, 68, 69, 70, 114; public

support for, 109; under Trump,
    115. *See also* globalization
Protestant Reformation, 30
Protestants, 44
Prussia, 48, 50, 51
Putin, Vladimir, 111, 125, 127, 129,
    130, 140

Quadruple Alliance, 48–49, 51
Quemoy and Matsu, 82

RAND Corporation, 125
Reagan, Ronald, 83
refugees, 139, 141
Regional Comprehensive
    Economic Project (RCEP), 124,
    131
revisionism: geopolitical, 6, 25, 38,
    56, 59, 95, 111, 127, 131, 136, 146,
    149–150, 155, 157, 158–159;
    historical, 60–61
Rhineland, 55, 61
Rice, Condoleezza, 102
Richelieu, Armand Jean du Plessis,
    Cardinal, 45–46
Roosevelt, Franklin, 67, 69, 70, 73,
    77, 78
Roosevelt, Theodore, 36
Russia, 56, 153; Chinese
    collaboration with, 128; under
    Concert system, 50; energy
    exports by, 120, 126;
    liberalization reversed in, 133;
    military buildup by, 121, 127;
    during Napoleonic Wars, 35,
    48–49; power reasserted by,
    125–126; sanctions against, 141;
    Syria allied with, 128–130, 134,
    140; Ukraine invaded by, 108,
    111–112, 125; U.S. vs., 94, 95,

103, 119, 127, 136, 150, 159; wars
    waged by, 29

Saudi Arabia, 128, 162
Schelling, Thomas, 159
Schiller, Friedrich, 145
Schroeder, Paul, 52
Scowcroft, Brent, 93
September 11 attacks, 94, 100,
    101–102
Sestanovich, Stephen, 161
Seven Against Thebes (Aeschylus),
    11–12
Seven Years' War (1756–1763), 32
Shanghai Cooperation
    Organization, 134
Sheehan, James, 39
social Darwinism, 36
"soft power," 135
Soleimani, Qassem, 127
Somalia, 94
Sophocles, 11, 12, 15, 27
South China Sea, 112, 123–124, 128,
    141, 142, 149, 159, 160
South Korea, 76, 78, 79, 87–88,
    142
South Ossetia, 130
sovereignty, 44–45, 139, 149, 159
Soviet Union, 98; as Cold War
    rival, 5, 66, 68–69, 74, 75, 79, 80,
    83, 84–85, 88, 90; collapse of, 92,
    97; League of Nations and, 56;
    totalitarianism in, 135
Spain, 30
Sparta, 7, 19, 20, 25–28, 84
Sputnik, 83
Stalin, Joseph, 133
Suppliant Women, The (Euripides),
    16–17
Sweden, 30

Syria, 108, 112, 126–130, 134, 137–139, 140

Taiwan, 125
Talleyrand, Charles Maurice de, 47
tariffs, 70–71
taxes, 104
terrorism, 95, 100, 138, 149, 162; in Europe, 139; public opinion toward, 109; U.S. policy toward, 94, 101, 110, 111, 136–137
Thebes, 17
Thirty Years' War (1618–1648), 29–32, 33, 42–44, 45, 47
Thucydides, 18–21, 26, 27–29, 144, 147
Toynbee, Arnold, 65
tragedy, 2–3; comic rendition of, 9–10; heroism seen in, 15; as inspiration, 22–40; lessons of, 4–5, 10–12, 18; as norm, 22–40; perils of, 52; rediscovering, 145–165; social and political functions of, 16; twin meanings of, 12; virtues of, 7–21
Trans-Pacific Partnership (TPP), 107, 141
Treaty of Versailles (1919), 53–54, 57
Trojan War, 15
Trotsky, Leon, 38
Truman, Harry, 73, 79; as internationalist, 67, 69, 71, 83, 87; Soviet threat and, 75–76, 78

Trump, Donald, 105, 107, 109, 112–116, 142–143
Turkey, 76, 79, 132
Twining, Daniel, 150

Ukraine, 108, 111–112, 125, 134, 160
unilateralism, 49, 50, 69, 77
United Arab Emirates, 128
United Nations, 78, 140

Vansittart, Robert Gilbert, Baron, 160
Venezuela, 132
Vietnam, 79, 83, 85–87, 95, 102, 124, 161, 162

War of the Spanish Succession (1701–1714), 32
Wells, H. G., 64
Wilson, Woodrow, 53–58, 70, 108
Wohlforth, William, 95, 120
Woolsey, James, 137
World Bank, 70, 77
World War I, 36–38, 52–55, 60–61
World War II, 38–40, 66–67, 77, 79, 83, 90, 92

Xerxes I, king of Persia, 13, 14
Xi Jinping, 131

Yang Jiechi, 123
Yeltsin, Boris, 140
Yemen, 127, 128